Dyslexia: A Very Short Introduction

'This engaging book gives a fascinating account of the processes involved in learning to read, and explains why it is an effortless achievement for most, but an epic struggle for some. The exceptional scholarship makes this book a precious resource for everything that research has revealed about dyslexia. It reveals how children learn to read and write, the cognitive requirements for this achievement, the brain processes involved, and evaluates the teaching approaches that work best. A must-read.'

Uta Frith, Emeritus Professor of Cognitive Development, UCL

'This is by far the best book written on dyslexia—conceptually incisive, balanced and thoughtful in approach, academically sound and extremely practical in the discussion of the implications for provision of services and for help for individuals. A masterpiece and a very interesting read as well.'

Michael Rutter, Professor of Developmental Psychopathology, KCL

VERY SHORT INTRODUCTIONS are for anyone wanting a stimulating and accessible way into a new subject. They are written by experts, and have been translated into more than 45 different languages.

The series began in 1995, and now covers a wide variety of topics in every discipline. The VSI library currently contains over 600 volumes—a Very Short Introduction to everything from Psychology and Philosophy of Science to American History and Relativity—and continues to grow in every subject area.

Very Short Introductions available now:

ABOLITIONISM Richard S. Newman
ACCOUNTING Christopher Nobes
ADAM SMITH Christopher J. Berry
ADOLESCENCE Peter K. Smith
ADVERTISING Winston Fletcher
AFRICAN AMERICAN RELIGION
   Eddie S. Glaude Jr
AFRICAN HISTORY John Parker
   and Richard Rathbone
AFRICAN POLITICS Ian Taylor
AFRICAN RELIGIONS
   Jacob K. Olupona
AGEING Nancy A. Pachana
AGNOSTICISM Robin Le Poidevin
AGRICULTURE Paul Brassley and
   Richard Soffe
ALEXANDER THE GREAT
   Hugh Bowden
ALGEBRA Peter M. Higgins
AMERICAN CULTURAL HISTORY
   Eric Avila
AMERICAN HISTORY Paul S. Boyer
AMERICAN IMMIGRATION
   David A. Gerber
AMERICAN LEGAL HISTORY
   G. Edward White
AMERICAN NAVAL HISTORY
   Craig L. Symonds
AMERICAN POLITICAL HISTORY
   Donald Critchlow
AMERICAN POLITICAL PARTIES
   AND ELECTIONS L. Sandy Maisel
AMERICAN POLITICS
   Richard M. Valelly

THE AMERICAN PRESIDENCY
   Charles O. Jones
THE AMERICAN REVOLUTION
   Robert J. Allison
AMERICAN SLAVERY
   Heather Andrea Williams
THE AMERICAN WEST Stephen Aron
AMERICAN WOMEN'S HISTORY
   Susan Ware
ANAESTHESIA Aidan O'Donnell
ANALYTIC PHILOSOPHY
   Michael Beaney
ANARCHISM Colin Ward
ANCIENT ASSYRIA Karen Radner
ANCIENT EGYPT Ian Shaw
ANCIENT EGYPTIAN ART AND
   ARCHITECTURE Christina Riggs
ANCIENT GREECE Paul Cartledge
THE ANCIENT NEAR EAST
   Amanda H. Podany
ANCIENT PHILOSOPHY Julia Annas
ANCIENT WARFARE
   Harry Sidebottom
ANGELS David Albert Jones
ANGLICANISM Mark Chapman
THE ANGLO-SAXON AGE John Blair
ANIMAL BEHAVIOUR
   Tristram D. Wyatt
THE ANIMAL KINGDOM
   Peter Holland
ANIMAL RIGHTS David DeGrazia
THE ANTARCTIC Klaus Dodds
ANTHROPOCENE Erle C. Ellis
ANTISEMITISM Steven Beller

Available soon:

For more information visit our website

www.oup.com/vsi/

Margaret J. Snowling

DYSLEXIA

A Very Short Introduction

OXFORD
UNIVERSITY PRESS

OXFORD
UNIVERSITY PRESS

Great Clarendon Street, Oxford, OX2 6DP,
United Kingdom

Oxford University Press is a department of the University of Oxford.
It furthers the University's objective of excellence in research, scholarship,
and education by publishing worldwide. Oxford is a registered trade mark of
Oxford University Press in the UK and in certain other countries

First edition published in 2019

Impression: 1

Published in the United States of America by Oxford University Press
198 Madison Avenue, New York, NY 10016, United States of America

British Library Cataloguing in Publication Data
Data available

Library of Congress Control Number: 2018968140

ISBN 978-0-19-881830-4

Printed in Great Britain by
Ashford Colour Press Ltd, Gosport, Hampshire

Contents

Acknowledgements

I am grateful to many friends and colleagues who have helped me distil the science of dyslexia into a very short introduction. My thanks are due to Silke Gobel, Bill Kirkup, Phil Kirby, Dianne Newbury, Denise Cripps, and Rob Wyke who read, commented on, and at times corrected the manuscript and Kate Nation and Dorothy Bishop who helped me fill in the gaps! I am extremely grateful to my graphic designer, Dean Chesher, and to Fumiko Hoeft, Sonali Nag, and Petra Hoffman who helped me source figures and Hermione Lee and Sophie Ratcliffe for encouragement. I was only able to complete the book with the support of St John's College, Oxford. My thanks to my hosts at Trinity College Dublin and the Australian Institute of Learning Sciences at ACU at which I spent some sabbatical leave and to the many children and families with dyslexia I have known and who inform this book. Charles Hulme accompanied me on my writing journey and as always provided support, feedback, and love for which I am ever grateful.

List of illustrations

Chapter 1
Does dyslexia exist?

Reading and writing are highly valued in almost all societies. Even as the use of technology for communications increases, this remains true: poor reading will always be a problem and there is no threat to the importance of literacy skills in daily life. Literacy skills are fundamental for formal education where so much of what we learn comes from printed texts. They are also part of the 'survival kit' which is needed to run our lives—when signing a lease, setting up a bank account, using an ATM, or reading a note sent home from school. It follows that difficulties with reading and writing have wide ranging effects beyond academic achievement: including effects on career opportunities, personal well-being, and to some extent mental health. Such difficulties are a problem not only for those affected, but also for society.

Literacy difficulties, when they are not caused by lack of education, are known as dyslexia. Dyslexia can be defined as a problem with learning which primarily affects the development of reading accuracy and fluency and spelling skills. Dyslexia frequently occurs together with other difficulties, such as problems in attention, organization, and motor skills (movement) but these are not in and of themselves indicators of dyslexia.

The difficulty which we now recognize as dyslexia was first described in the English-speaking world in 1896 by William

Pringle Morgan, a general practitioner writing in the *British Medical Journal*. He wrote of a 14-year-old patient, Percy (which the boy spelled *Precy*), who was a 'bright and intelligent boy, quick at games, and in no way inferior to others of his age. His great difficulty has been—and is now—his inability to learn to read.' Following examination of Percy, who had no eye or visual defects and a good education to date, Pringle Morgan concluded that this was a case of *congenital word blindness*: literally the inability to store the visual images of words in memory. He hypothesized that it must be due to defective development of a region of the brain called the left angular gyrus. Interestingly, the boy was able to read figures normally and enjoyed arithmetic, so his problems appeared to be specific to literacy. Looking back, it is interesting how fitting this description was. As we shall see, it is now widely held that dyslexia is a specific learning disorder. However, there is continuing debate regarding the boundaries of the 'disorder', its precise characterization, and even its name.

Before we begin, we will look at three cases which place the story of dyslexia into a contemporary context. We will refer back to these cases frequently, to illustrate the many features of this developmental condition and our understanding of it.

Bobby

Bobby is a 7-year-old boy who is verbally bright but struggling to learn to read. He is the first child in his family and although he was a late-talker his parents did not worry because he was very communicative. When Bobby began to talk, he was difficult to understand and the family were often amused by the strange words he 'made up' to refer to things. It was only when Bobby went to school that his difficulties became obvious. Although he had known some letters and even some words in preschool, he had not been able to master phonics. He did not do at all well in the phonics checks conducted by his teacher at the end of Year 1, and

*his writing, although well formed, was minimal and his spellings
mostly difficult to decipher. He was placed in a special 'catch-up'
group in his class in an attempt to bring his reading on and,
although classmates in the same group progressed well, Bobby did
not. Rather he began to fall further and further behind his peers
and his behaviour began to deteriorate.*

Misha

*Misha is a 10-year-old girl who has struggled with reading since
starting school. Her parents are worried because she will soon be
transferring to secondary school and they fear she will not be able
to cope with the literacy demands. Misha has received two lots of
intervention (remedial reading) within school and has progressed
quite well in both reading and writing. However, her reading is
still slow and effortful. Because she has to expend a lot of energy
on decoding words on the page, she finds it difficult also to pay
attention to what she is reading; not surprisingly, she gets little
enjoyment from reading. Misha is very creative and loves writing
and illustrating stories. In fact this is one of her favourite
pastimes. Yet her spelling is poor and she does not get credit for
what is, in all other respects, excellent work. Misha is becoming
increasingly anxious about her performance and beginning to say
she doesn't want to go to school.*

Harry

*Harry is a 30-year-old man who has made his career in the food
industry, primarily in marketing. He has great ideas for branding
and advertising and he is a superb salesman. Harry says that he
has struggled academically throughout his life. He was assessed
for dyslexia at 9 years of age and had a lot of extra help with
reading and spelling, both from his parents and from a tutor. As a
young adult, he avoids literacy-related tasks—indeed that is why
he has chosen to be a salesman—but he struggles to complete forms,
invoices, and tax returns. Harry avoids reading at all costs,*

saying he has only ever read one book (Like a Virgin by Richard
Branson). He writes when he has to—mainly lists: lists of things
to do and not to forget! He would say that it is his memory and
organizational skills which let him down most—not his literacy.

These three cases provide a sense of what it is like to be dyslexic.
The nature of dyslexia changes with age and the 'symptoms'
experienced appear to shift, too. Nonetheless, at the core of the
problem is a difficulty in *decoding* words for reading and *encoding*
them for spelling. Fluency in these processes is never achieved.
Further, the condition persists in spite of the provision of 'extra
help'. The three cases also illustrate co-occurring problems:
for Bobby some conduct difficulties; for Misha, anxiety; and for
Harry, problems of memory, attention, and organization. Such
additional difficulties are common, but whether they are a
consequence of dyslexia or have a different origin is not yet
fully understood.

The medical model of dyslexia

During the early years of the 20th century, the study of congenital
word blindness was taken up by eye specialists like James
Hinshelwood, a contemporary of William Pringle Morgan, who
described cases adhering to what was to become the 'medical
model' of dyslexia. These clinicians viewed 'congenital word
blindness' as a discrete condition with a specific set of signs and
symptoms. However, this conceptualization of reading difficulties
began to change in the 1930s following the landmark publication
Disorders of Speech, Language, Reading and Spelling by the
American neuropathologist, Dr Samuel T. Orton.

Orton had a very important insight: he noticed that poor reading
runs in families *and* that other family members often have
problems of speech or language, including stammering. He went
on to link these observations to incomplete *brain lateralization*
(the tendency of one side of the brain to specialize in certain

cognitive functions) and, in turn, with the frequent letter and word reversals associated with dyslexia. Since visual information was understood to arrive in the dominant hemisphere in the correct orientation while the exact mirror image was received in the non-dominant hemisphere, it was important to suppress the confusing image if reading was to proceed normally. He believed a child who had not established brain dominance would be unable to suppress the mirror image and there would be continuing confusion between symbols, particularly reversible ones like 'b' and 'd'. He used the term *'strephosymbolia'*, literally twisting of symbols, to describe the condition. While his theory was incorrect, as is the related idea that dyslexia is associated with left handedness, his observations about family traits hold true and, as will be shown, these do indeed help us to understand the causal pathways that lead to dyslexia (see Figure 1).

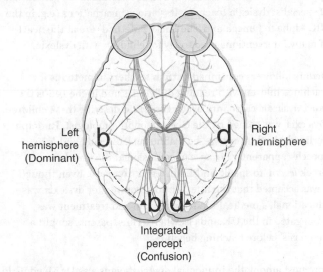

1. Schematic representation of Orton's hypothesis that a lack of brain dominance led to confusion between visual images projected on to the left and right sides of the brain.

However, Orton has been remembered not for his theory but for the practice which originated in his clinic in Boston in the 1930s. Here two talented educators, Anna Gillingham and Bessie Stillman, pioneered methods for remediating reading difficulties. They worked from the assumption that the cause of reading difficulties was the failure to memorize the sequences of letters in words; so, the task was to establish memory representations for these, without having to rely on (faulty) visual processes. The approach they developed uses all three sensory modalities—visual, auditory, and kinaesthetic (movement)—to reinforce new concepts during learning and to circumvent the basic deficit, a strategy described as 'multisensory teaching'. But the approach involves much more. Children are taught explicitly how the writing system works by mapping letters and letter sequences to sounds, thereby building up knowledge of letter–sound correspondences, spelling patterns, and rules. The successful Orton–Gillingham–Stillman approach is still known worldwide and has influenced generations of specialist dyslexia teachers. Its various incarnations (e.g. in the UK, Alpha to Omega and The Hickey Method) are at the heart of many interventions used today for children with dyslexia.

Orton's followers continued to train teachers in methods for teaching children with reading difficulties and in the 1960s the word 'dyslexia' came into use in the UK to describe these children. 'Dyslexia' was coined by the German ophthalmologist, Rudolph Berlin, derived from *dys-* 'bad, abnormal, difficult' and *lexis* 'speech' (apparently because of confusion at the time between Greek *legein* 'to speak' and Latin *legere* 'to read'). Even though it was accepted that the intervention required for dyslexia was educational, a medical model of referral and treatment was propagated in the UK and elsewhere. Thus, parents sought a 'diagnosis' before teaching began.

Foremost among the influential diagnosticians was Dr Macdonald Critchley, a neurologist at the National Hospital in London who saw children in his clinic and subsequently 'referred' them for treatment. In 1963, just around the corner from this clinic, the Word Blind Centre opened, bringing together a team comprising doctors, psychologists, teachers, and speech therapists to assess and teach dyslexic children. Among those working in the centre were two pioneers, Professor Tim Miles and Dr Sandhya Naidoo, who each wrote an influential book which would take dyslexia research in a more scientific direction. The Word Blind Centre became known for its expertise and parents would travel many miles to have their children assessed and to receive special lessons, usually once a week.

Despite these advances, dyslexia began to attract a reputation as a disorder of the middle classes and, increasingly, its existence was dismissed by education professionals. This was a sorry state of affairs. It was true that it was primarily more educated parents who found their way to centres which would 'diagnose dyslexia' but this was more about those parents' awareness of the condition than about their children's needs. Regrettably the needs of children with severe reading and spelling difficulties were often neglected. What was required was a study using robust methodology which could characterize such children and assess their response to teaching. A study of the health, education, and behaviour of all 9- to 10-year-olds living on the Isle of Wight during the 1960s provided such evidence.

Dyslexia or specific learning disorder?

The Isle of Wight population study was ground-breaking. All 2,334 of the 9–11-year-old children living on the island were surveyed using a wide variety of measures. The aim was to establish the prevalence of childhood disorders of health and well-being, including psychiatric conditions and learning disorders. As part of this large study, Michael Rutter, Bill Yule, and their colleagues assessed the children's educational attainments and related them to IQ. This procedure allowed the differentiation of children with low levels of reading attainment commensurate with lower levels of cognitive ability, from children with more specific difficulties (who were, at that time, considered to be dyslexic).

It is important to describe some features of the methods they used. All children were assessed using the *Wechsler Intelligence Scale for Children* (WISC) which provides measures of verbal, non-verbal (performance), and full-scale IQ. The children also completed a reading assessment in which they read aloud short passages and answered questions they were asked about them. The test provided measures of reading accuracy, reading rate, and reading comprehension. There was a moderately strong relationship between IQ and reading attainment in the sample (a correlation of about 0.6)—in other words, children of higher ability were typically better at reading (in terms of both accuracy and comprehension). The researchers then applied a statistical approach using data from the population sample to predict the expected reading attainment of every child, given their IQ. Once these 'expected' scores had been derived it was possible to compare them with the actual scores the children obtained and, then, to identify children whose attained reading score fell significantly below expectation. The children so identified had *specific* reading difficulties (described at the time as 'specific reading retardation'). The critical question was: did these children look like those described by the medical model as dyslexic?

To answer this question, the research team compared the children with specific reading difficulties with equally poor readers from the sample but in this case those whose poor reading was in line with expectation, given their lower cognitive ability (we will call them low-ability poor readers). To put it another way, to investigate the concept of dyslexia they compared 'unexpectedly' poor readers with 'expectedly' poor readers.

The findings from this comparison were salutary. There were relatively few differences between the children with specific reading difficulties and the children who were low-ability poor readers—it wasn't that one group looked 'dyslexic' and the other group just 'slow'. Indeed, there was no evidence to support the 'soft neurological signs' agreed to be associated with dyslexia by a meeting of *The World Congress of Neurology* in 1968. Nevertheless, the group differences were informative. Among children with specific reading difficulties, more boys were affected than girls (a ratio of about 3:1) and a history of delays and difficulties with speech and language was common in this group. In contrast, approximately equal numbers of boys and girls were low-ability poor readers and they had experienced a wide range of developmental delays and difficulties, not only with speech and language but also in motor coordination.

Arguably of most importance, the progress of the two groups over two years differed: a follow-up study revealed that the children with specific reading problems had actually made *less* progress in basic reading skills than the low-ability poor readers, despite being of higher intelligence. Thus, the Isle of Wight study presented some of the earliest evidence that children with specific reading difficulties show a poor response to reading instruction. In more recent times, 'response to intervention' has been proposed as a better way of identifying likely dyslexic difficulties than measured reading skills. And as we shall see, the approach to defining reading problems on the basis of a discrepancy between IQ and reading attainment has fallen from favour.

Dyslexia defies definition

The findings of the Isle of Wight study were influential in clarifying the fact that the problem of specific reading difficulties was a real one. In Britain the term 'specific learning difficulties' came into being while 'learning disabilities' was used in the US. But what became of the concept of dyslexia? A Google search for the term 'dyslexia' receives 11 million hits, 'specific learning difficulties' half as many. Indeed, the definition of dyslexia continues to be debated though the term remains in general use. To this day, there is tension between the medical model of 'dyslexia' and the understanding of 'specific learning difficulties' in educational circles.

The nub of the problem for the concept of dyslexia is that, unlike measles or chicken pox, it is not a disorder with a clear diagnostic profile. Rather, reading skills are distributed normally in the population (a statistical term, meaning that reading, like weight or height, varies continuously, with the majority of people being in the average range) and there is no boundary between 'dyslexia' and 'normal' reading. Nonetheless, if children have difficulties decoding print this will be an obstacle to reading with understanding which, in turn, is a significant barrier to educational achievement.

So we can ask: why does the concept of dyslexia survive? One reason is that there are many children who struggle significantly with learning to read and write and who require educational support. And there are many reports that without this support these children experience a downward spiral of low achievement and poor self-esteem, perhaps leading also to the issues with emotional and behavioural adjustment observed in the three cases introduced earlier. The point of 'labelling' these children, then, is to communicate their educational needs and to provide interventions—basically, to flag the need for an intervention to support their literacy skills. Moreover, since learning disorders persist across the life span, the dyslexia label can signal the need for appropriate arrangements to be put in place not just at school but also in the workplace. Indeed, it is important to ensure that people such as Harry do not struggle with the literacy demands associated with a career to which they are otherwise well suited.

In this respect, dyslexia is like high blood pressure. There is no precise cut-off between high blood pressure and 'normal' blood pressure, but if high blood pressure remains untreated, the risk of complications is high. Hence, a diagnosis of 'hypertension' is warranted and this, in turn, leads to recommendations of medication (and possibly other interventions). There is not the same approach to thinking about dyslexia; there are no agreed cut-off criteria and few evidence-based treatments. However, this book will show that there is remarkable agreement among researchers regarding the risk factors for poor reading and a growing number of evidence-based interventions: dyslexia definitely exists and we can do a great deal to ameliorate its effects (see Figure 2).

2. Dyslexia 'welcome' cartoon.

Chapter 2
How to learn to read (or not)

The aim of much research on dyslexia was to discover what causes this perplexing learning difficulty in people like Bobby, Misha, and Harry. Before we can address this issue, we need to lay out the stages through which a child must progress on the journey to literacy so that we can consider its demands. Our three cases, Bobby, Misha, and Harry, are all English and have been taught to read in their native language. Since most research on reading development has been conducted in English, English will be our primary focus. We will use evidence from scientific studies to develop a theoretical background against which to consider the universal aspects of learning to read and then aspects that are specific to different languages.

Learning to read: a developmental framework

In most countries, including those with less advanced education systems, formal reading instruction begins when children enter school. However, literacy development starts long before this, particularly in families who value literacy. An obvious though not often acknowledged fact is that literacy builds on a foundation of spoken language—indeed, an assumption of all education systems is that, when a child starts school, their spoken language is sufficient to support reading development. In addition, pre-reading skills frequently form part of the preschool curriculum. Thus, many children start school with considerable knowledge about books: they know that print runs from left to right (at least if you are reading English) and that you read from the front to the back of the book; and they are familiar with at least some letter names or sounds.

At a basic level, reading involves translating printed symbols into pronunciations—a task referred to as decoding, which requires mapping across modalities from vision (written forms) to audition (spoken sounds). Beyond knowing letters, the beginning reader has to discover how printed words relate to spoken words and a major aim of reading instruction is to help the learner to 'crack' this code. To decode in English (and other alphabetic languages) requires learning about 'grapheme–phoneme' correspondences—literally the way in which letters or letter combinations relate to the speech sounds of spoken words: this is not a trivial task. When children use language naturally, they have only implicit knowledge of the words they use and they do not pay attention to their sounds; but this is precisely what they need to do in order to learn to decode. Indeed, they have to become 'aware' that words can be broken down into constituent parts like the syllable ('*buttercup*' = /but/-/ur/-/kup/) and that, in turn, syllables can be segmented into phonemes ('*cup*' = /k/-/u/-/p/). Phonemes are the smallest sounds which differentiate words; for example, '*pit*' and '*bit*' differ by a single phoneme [b]-[p] (in fact, both are referred to as 'stop consonants' and they differ only by a single phonemic feature, namely the timing of the voicing onset of the consonant). In the English writing system, phonemes are the units which are coded in the grapheme-correspondences that make up the orthographic code.

Acquiring the alphabetic principle

The term 'phoneme awareness' refers to the ability to reflect on and manipulate the speech sounds in words. It is a metalinguistic skill (a skill requiring conscious control of language) which develops after the ability to segment words into syllables and into rhyming parts (like the [oat] sound in 'goat'). There has been controversy over whether phoneme awareness is a cause or a consequence of learning to read. The observation that adults who are illiterate cannot perform phoneme awareness tasks suggests it is a consequence of reading but the evidence is by no means conclusive. In children, the debate has focused on whether children learn letters before they become aware of the phonemes they represent or whether, in contrast, phoneme awareness and letter knowledge have separate origins. The correct interpretation is likely to be a mix of the two; the development of letter knowledge and explicit awareness of phonemes can proceed separately and there is also evidence of reciprocal interactions, with one skill influencing the development of the other as reading proceeds. In general, letters are easier to learn (being concrete) than phoneme awareness is to acquire (being an abstract skill).

To illustrate some of the challenges the child faces in learning to read, Brian Byrne conducted an ingenious series of experiments. The children, preschoolers who could not yet read, were taught the written forms of pairs of words like *hat-hats* and *book-books*. Once they had learned these words, they could generalize their newly acquired knowledge to read '*dogs*' given '*dog*'. However, it was only those who knew the sound of the letter 's' that could read '*bus*' given '*bug*'. Similarly, after teaching the comparative '*er*' to make a word like '*small*' -> '*smaller*', the children without letter-sound knowledge could read '*meaner*' given '*mean*' but could not read '*corner*' if given '*corn*'. These simple illustrations highlight the abstract nature of the phonological coding of words—when children come to the task of learning, they exhibit a natural semantic bias towards meaning and they need to override this in order to decode.

The acquisition of 'phoneme awareness' is a critical step in the development of decoding skills. A typical reader who possesses both letter knowledge *and* phoneme awareness can readily 'sound out' letters and blend the sounds together to read words or even meaningless but pronounceable letter strings (nonwords); conversely, they can split up words (segment them) into sounds for spelling. When these building blocks are in place, a child has developed 'alphabetic competence' and the task of becoming a reader can begin properly. In a neat demonstration of the influence of alphabetic subskills on these initial steps into reading, we used data from an intervention study in which 4–5-year-old children were taught letters and trained in phoneme awareness to investigate increases in decoding (The Nuffield Language for Reading Project). The results of this study showed that the gains the children made in letter knowledge and phoneme awareness together predicted gains in word decoding, suggesting a causal influence from these basic building blocks to reading.

Our case, Bobby, faltered at this initial stage of learning to read. Although he knew some letters and even some words, he was slow to develop phoneme awareness (possibly because of his earlier speech problems), he struggled to grasp the alphabetic principle, and he could not master the basics of decoding written words, often called 'phonics'. Even at this early stage he started to avoid reading and getting him to practise was a struggle for his parents who were eager to help.

Becoming a fluent reader

In her classic 'stage' model, Linnea Ehri described the transition to reading fluency as the move from the 'alphabetic' to the 'orthographic' stage of reading. The child no longer needs to sound out the units of words to achieve pronunciation and meaning but begins to form mental images of words which can be immediately accessed from memory for reading and spelling. To explain how a child comes to build up a mental dictionary (or 'lexicon') of words, David Share and others have suggested the idea of phonological decoding as the 'sine qua non of reading acquisition', that is, the indispensable skill. According to this view, learning to read involves the growth of a lexicon to which words are added item by item after they have been decoded. In turn, the phonological decoding process gradually becomes 'lexicalized' (embedding orthographic knowledge as it is abstracted) and hence more proficient for decoding novel words. Furthermore, if the results of a decoding attempt are ambiguous or partial (e.g. reading 'island' as [iz-land]), top–down knowledge from the sentence level and from the child's vocabulary is brought into play to arrive at the correct pronunciation and thus learn the word.

The self-teaching hypothesis has spurred a large amount of research using a standard experimental set-up. Basically, children are exposed to new words which they haven't seen before, e.g. *'yate'* (either in a story context or in isolation). After a delay, they are asked to select the previously experienced words from a selection of alternative 'foils'. By carefully creating the foils to closely resemble the target words either visually (e.g. *'yafe'*), or phonologically (e.g. *'yait'*), it is possible to tell whether or not the child has remembered the precise spelling of the target word—its orthographic form. A further critical test is to ask the child to spell the new word. Researchers have used this procedure to examine the effects of context, frequency of exposure, and time delay on performance, and to compare good and poor readers. It is now known that learning the precise orthographic form of a word is sometimes possible after decoding it only once, but more generally, learning increases with an increasing number of exposures and it depends on the phonological skills of the reader.

Another factor which is important in promoting reading fluency is the size of a child's vocabulary. In English, vocabulary is particularly important for learning exception words which do not conform to grapheme–phoneme correspondence rules: words like *'aunt'*, *'glove'*, or *'broad'*. Kate Nation and I were the first to show that children's vocabulary knowledge predicted differences in their ability to read such irregular words. In turn, we showed that children with poor oral language skills, specifically limited semantic knowledge of words, had particular difficulty in reading irregular words. Their problems stood out in contrast to the relative ease with which they read regular words or nonwords devoid of meaning.

Consideration of the role of vocabulary in reading irregular words may suggest that words are committed to lexical memory one by one as whole meaning units. However, this does not seem to be the case. Rather children appear to be able to use the meaning relationships between words to decipher unknown forms. The smallest unit of meaning is the morpheme; morphemes can be combined to change word meaning and grammatical class. For example, the word '*happiness*' is a combination of the morpheme '*happy*' and the suffix '*ness*' which make the adjective '*happy*' into a noun. Similarly, adding the prefix '*un*' changes its meaning from '*happy*' to '*unhappy*'. Understanding the morphological structure of language—'morphological awareness'—is thought to foster reading fluency and support reading comprehension. It is particularly important in English where morphology may lead to inconsistencies in spelling (e.g. the relationship between '*autumn*' and '*autumnal*' in which the 'n' is silent in the noun and voiced in the adjective).

A division of labour?

It is worth pausing here to reflect on individual differences in reading. According to the 'interactive compensatory' model of reading, 'bottom–up' reading processes (such as phonological decoding) interact with 'top–down' processes (such as hypothesis testing guided by context) to account for variation in reading fluency. Thus, top–down processes constrain lower-level analyses and lower-level analyses constrain top–down processes in order to achieve precision in reading. Furthermore, compensation is possible in that top–down processes can aid or 'bootstrap' decoding when it is inefficient or poorly developed and bottom–up processes can fill in the 'gaps' remaining when semantic strategies are used to guide reading. In other words, when faced with a word they cannot read, children can often use the other words around it to help read or understand it.

Much of the evidence for the interactive–compensatory model comes from experiments using priming tasks. Priming, as the name suggests, is getting something ready for action, in this case, the reading response. In a priming task, the reader is shown a target word like 'nurse' in one of two conditions: either in a neutral context (e.g. *'young'* <u>nurse</u>) or in a semantic context (e.g. *'doctor'* <u>nurse</u>). The time to read the target '<u>nurse</u>' is measured in the two cases. As expected, *'nurse'* can be read more quickly following the related word *'doctor'* than following the unrelated word *'young'*. This is known as the 'semantic facilitation' or 'priming' effect. The facilitation effect is larger for readers with dyslexia than for good readers. At first this might seem surprising. However, because poor readers are slow to decode, this allows more time for context to have an effect. But in addition, it depends upon their vocabulary knowledge. It is only when this is good that context will have a beneficial effect; for 'doctor' to prime 'nurse' you have to know the meanings of both words.

Our case Misha appears to have had difficulty in making the transition to fluent reading. However, she is able to read accurately albeit slowly. Her vocabulary is good and so is her comprehension of language—it is tempting to suggest that she is using top–down strategies that rely on such language skills to bootstrap her ineffective decoding. Perhaps this is also why she is not good at spelling. Over-reliance on higher-order language processes works against the development of the detailed memory representations needed for accurate spelling. Nonetheless, the idea that top–down processes can influence word-level reading is important. Such processes rely on a range of language and conceptual processes which go beyond the phonological (speech-based) processes that are at the heart of early reading development and include vocabulary. Typically, such processes are considered important for reading comprehension but they are rarely considered in relation to the growth of word reading.

Thus, within the interactive compensatory framework, there is interaction between the phonological processes used to decode and the semantic attributes of words that are also involved in word reading. In a similar vein, Mark Seidenberg and colleagues have argued for a division of labour between two pathways in learning to read, phonology and semantics (see Figure 3). Essentially, reading is a 'big data' problem—the task of learning involves extracting the statistical relationships between spelling (orthography) and sound (phonology) and using these to develop an algorithm for reading which is continually refined as further words are encountered. Seidenberg and colleagues have implemented this idea in a computer programme, the 'triangle' model, which simulates the process of reading development. It is called the 'triangle' model because it creates connections not only between phonological and orthographic units but also with the meanings of words (morphemes) via a semantic pathway (though this part of the model has not been fully implemented).

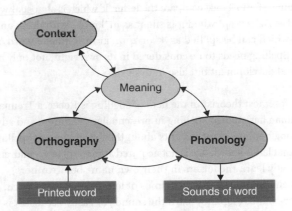

3. Seidenberg and McClelland's (1989) 'triangle' model of reading.

In the initial stages of reading, the focus is on establishing mappings between phonology and orthography (akin to phonological decoding in children) and later the focus turns to more direct mappings between orthography and meaning. In the dual-route model, there are separate routes, one the phonological route that translates graphemes into phonemes, and a more direct lexical route from a lexicon of word-level orthographic forms to their pronunciations. While in recent implementations of the model there is interaction between the two systems, its implications for development have seldom been explored.

Learning to spell

Spelling has been the 'Cinderella' of reading research. It is commonly believed that spelling is simply the reverse of reading. It is not. As a consequence, learning to read does not always bring with it spelling proficiency. One reason is that the correspondences between letters and sounds used for reading (grapheme–phoneme correspondences) are not just the same as the sound-to-letter rules used for writing (phoneme–grapheme correspondences). Indeed, in English, the correspondences used in reading are generally more consistent than those used in spelling—for instance compare the letter 'k' which is almost always read as /k/ (except when it is silent as in 'know') with the sound [k] which can be spelled as 'k' or 'c' or, at the end of a word, as 'ck'. Spelling needs to be considered in its own right, not only in typical development but also in dyslexia.

The foremost theorist in the field of spelling is Rebecca Treiman. Treiman has studied spelling in preschoolers, children, and adults. Among her important insights about the foundations of spelling are that letter knowledge is not acquired at random (e.g. children typically learn the letters in their own name before others), that children often use the names of letters in order to learn letter-sounds (e.g. they learn the sound /b/ easily because it is the first phoneme in the name of 'B' [bee], compared with /h/ which is not in the sound of the name 'H' ['aitch']) and that children learn a lot about orthography and orthographic conventions through informal encounters with print before they begin to read (such as not writing 'mm' at the beginning of words). The message is that spelling concepts develop early and provide an entrée to the process of becoming a writer.

As is the case for reading, learning to spell requires the child to be aware of the phonemic structure of spoken words. Children's early spelling attempts reveal that they are attuned to the phonetic structure of words (how they are articulated) rather than to their visual structure. Some of the classic errors made by pre-literate children include writing 'train' as CHAN and 'dragon' as JAGN. Although incorrect, these spellings certainly capture something of the sound of the target word. In fact, many of the early spelling errors children make replicate errors observed in speech development: consonant clusters are often reduced at the beginning ('clap'→ CAP; step → TEP) and the end ('lamp' → LAP; 'tent' → TET) of words, dropping unstressed syllables is common ('balloon' → BLOON; 'caterpillar' → CATPILLA; 'elephant' → LFANT) as is merging words together in writing. Notably, the salient sounds of words are usually retained (e.g. 'back' → BK).

Detailed analyses of the nature of children's spelling errors can provide a sort of window on the development of their phonological (speech–sound) skills. Children with dyslexia often struggle to spell words phonetically as the writing samples from two children with dyslexia aged 9 and 14 years show (see Figure 4). The first from child TB is a piece of free writing; the piece from BB was written in five minutes in response to the prompt 'write a letter to an architect describing your dream home'. The children show differing levels of phonological proficiency; TB's writing is phonologically inaccurate and hence very difficult to decipher; in contrast, BB has better phonological awareness and his errors are phonologically accurate (so that they can be read back easily).

to the cods bopd done fleeing at then the grmnees
1 a solidle d at wos the wo spraor up

TB age 9

I would like it ⚡ to be worn ~~and hammy~~
Kleen and in a close with a glat ~~to~~ garden
with a alar. I would like it to be in a small village
with no bissy car.

BB age 14

4. Examples of dyslexic writing from children aged 9 and 14 years: BB's spelling is phonetically acceptable, TB's is not.

The relationship between phoneme awareness and letter knowledge at age 4 and phonological accuracy of spelling attempts at age 5 has been studied longitudinally with the aim of understanding individual differences in children's spelling skills. As expected, these two components of alphabetic knowledge predicted the phonological accuracy of children's early spelling. In turn, children's phonological spelling accuracy along with their reading skill at this early stage predicted their spelling proficiency after three years in school. The findings suggest that the ability to transcode phonologically provides a foundation for the development of orthographic representations for spelling but this alone is not enough—information acquired from reading experience is required to ensure spellings are conventionally correct. Misha had not inferred this information and this is one reason why she continued to be a poor speller through her primary school years.

Once the basic building blocks of spelling are in place, the child must build up detailed knowledge of the mappings from sounds to symbols that are specific to the writing system. In English, these mappings are more consistent between letter strings and the rhyme units of spoken words (e.g. /oat/ → -OAT; /eat/ → -EAT) than between phonemes and graphemes where several choices are often possible (e.g. the spelling of /E/ can be one of the following: EE; EA; EI; IE; EY; Y etc.). Like adults, children are sensitive to the consistency of spelling–sound correspondences; to some extent they can abstract the mappings implicitly but it is clear that formal instruction in spelling plays a part, particularly when it comes to learning how to spell vowels like /E/ or /I/.

Beyond phonology, children must also bring other sources of linguistic knowledge to bear in their spelling, notably grammar and morphology. It will be recalled that morphology refers to the ways in which words are formed and how they relate to meanings. Morphemes can signal grammatical relationships, such as the past tense *-ed*, and the progressive *-ing*, or meaning relationships, such as *sign–sign*ature. Treiman and colleagues showed how children's knowledge of morphology can sometimes override phonological knowledge in an intriguing experiment in which American children were asked to spell words containing 'taps'. A tap is a quick flap of the tongue just behind the upper teeth which sounds more like a voiced /d/ sound in words like *'city'* and *'eater'* than the voiceless /t/ more commonly used in England. American children are more likely to choose to spell a tap sound with a 'd' than a 't'. However, in words like *'eater'*, where the tap is at a morphological boundary between word stem (*eat*) and affix (*-er*), they are much more likely to use 't'. In contrast, they stick with 'd' for *'city'*, a word which contains only one morpheme.

Young children quickly grasp how grammatical knowledge dictates spelling choice. They soon learn that the past tense is usually written as *'ed'* and not as 't' which is how it sounds in most contexts (e.g. *'slipped'*); later they may use knowledge of the morphological structure of words to aid the spelling of some irregular words (e.g. using *'magic'* to spell *'magician'*). In addition, there are writing conventions which depend upon linguistic rules which have to be learned (such as when to use an apostrophe).

23

A wealth of data on the development of spelling has been brought together in the Integration of Multiple Patterns Framework. According to this framework, children are more likely to use a given spelling when multiple sources of evidence suggest this is the correct usage. They find it harder to produce the correct spelling when there is conflicting information. Like the triangle model of reading, this theory has at its heart the importance of learning the statistical regularities between the printed forms of words, their sounds, and meanings.

Finally, for spelling as for reading, practice is important. Indeed, there is some evidence that the kinaesthetic feedback associated with writing (how it feels to write) might be an important factor which aids learning by reinforcing the movement patterns underlying spelling. Writing is, of course, fundamentally a motor skill and it is not only about spelling but also about composing. There is too little knowledge of how writing develops, the role it plays in learning to spell, and how writing may be compromised in poor spellers: these are important issues for future research to explore.

Reading for meaning

To this point, our focus has been on learning to identify words: we have considered reading as a decoding process and spelling as encoding. However, the ultimate goal is literacy and to become literate requires more than reading and writing single words. Let us digress to consider reading comprehension using a classic framework known as the *Simple View of Reading*.

According to the Simple View of Reading, reading comprehension (R) is the product of decoding (D) and linguistic or language comprehension (L): R=D*L. Because reading comprehension is the *product* of these two components, it is not possible without proficiency in each. So, when children are still learning to decode, their understanding of text will be constrained by limitations in decoding, regardless of their language skills; conversely reading comprehension will also be limited if a child has poor oral language comprehension, even if their ability to decode is very good.

Consistent with this framework, studies have shown that, in the early stages of learning to read, reading comprehension is highly dependent on decoding skills: you cannot understand print that you cannot decode. However, as decoding skills increase so does reading comprehension; in turn, it begins to depend more upon language comprehension. In adulthood, reading and listening comprehension are virtually indistinguishable (the correlation between these skills is above 0.9). For reasons of space, and because dyslexia is primarily a problem with word recognition, we cannot spend long discussing the range of skills required for satisfactory text comprehension. For those who are interested the review *Ending the Reading Wars: From Novice to Expert* provides a comprehensive synthesis bridging what is known about learning to read and reading to learn.

From a slightly different perspective, the Lexical Quality Hypothesis offers a way of thinking about how the different attributes of words are brought together in the reading system of the fluent reader in the service of reading meaning. Central to this theory is the notion of 'lexical efficiency'—the ability to rapidly identify words because they have representations that are well specified in terms of spelling, meaning, and pronunciation. Within this model, the lexicons of skilled readers are furnished with more and higher-quality representations than those of less skilled readers. Quality may be compromised for different reasons, including poor phonological, orthographic, or semantic knowledge or skills. Regardless, the consequence of low lexical quality is that word reading is slow and error prone, meaning that less time and fewer cognitive resources are available to get on with the important job of text comprehension. For poor readers with fewer high-quality representations, reading comprehension is inevitably compromised (even when compensation is at work).

The Lexical Quality Hypothesis clarifies that, while reading comprehension depends upon decoding and language comprehension, an outcome of the two skills developing together is the development of high-quality lexical representations of words which, in turn, foster more fluency in word reading and better reading comprehension. In the longer term, readers with poorly specified lexical representations can gain little pleasure from reading and, for many, this means they are not motivated to read. The consequence is a low level of print exposure and ultimately poor literacy. In turn, this may limit increases in vocabulary size that normally accompany literacy, referred to as a 'Matthew Effect'.

Learning to read in different languages

So far I have presented what has been referred to as an 'Anglocentric' perspective on learning to read. What about learning to read in a language other than English? Which aspects of the process are the same and which different? Irrespective of the language, reading involves mapping between the visual symbols of words and their phonological forms. What differs between languages is the nature of the symbols and the phonological units. Indeed, the mappings which need to be created are at different levels of 'grain size' in different languages (fine-grained in alphabets which connect letters and sounds like German or Italian, and more coarse-grained in logographic systems like Chinese that map between characters and syllabic units). Languages also differ in the complexity of their morphology and how this maps to the orthography.

Among the alphabetic languages, English is the least regular, particularly for spelling; the most regular is Finnish with a completely transparent system of mappings between letters and phonemes (though words are generally long and embed several morphological units). The term 'orthographic depth' is used to describe the level of regularity which is observed between languages—English is opaque (or deep), followed by Danish and

French which also contain many irregularities, while Spanish and Italian rank among the more regular, transparent (or shallow) orthographies.

Over the years, there has been much discussion as to whether children learning to read English have a particularly tough task and there is frequent speculation that dyslexia is more prevalent in English than in other languages. There is no evidence that this is the case. But what is clear is that it takes longer to become a fluent reader of English than of a more transparent language; a large-scale cross-linguistic study conducted by Philip Seymour and his colleagues in the 1990s showed that, in the more transparent languages, children in the first grade of school are already accurate more than 90 per cent of the time when decoding words; in English it is 40 per cent.

More recently, the ELDEL Project (Enhancing Literacy Development in European Languages) studied the reading development of children learning to read in five European languages: English, French, Spanish, Czech, and Slovak. Figure 5

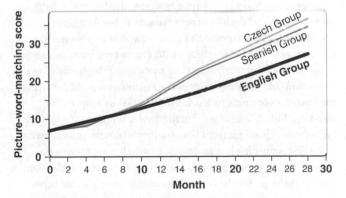

5. Growth of reading skill in children learning to read in English, Spanish, and Czech (note: formal instruction begins a year earlier in England and Wales).

shows the growth trajectory of reading skills in English compared to the more regular Spanish and Czech over the first school years. Bearing in mind that the English children in the UK started formal reading instruction a year before the Spanish and Czech children, the differences are striking.

The graph shows that performance on a timed reading task which assessed picture–word matching follows a slowly rising upward trajectory in the English children from age 4 (month 0) to age 6½ years (month 30). For the Spanish and Czech children, the pattern is different. They follow the same trajectory as the English children for the first year; then, when reading instruction begins around month 8, there is a sharp upward rise in trajectory indicating a 'growth spurt'; this is followed by some slowing as word reading fluency continues to develop. It is also notable that from around 16 months the growth in reading fluency is similar in the three languages with the English children remaining at a lower level throughout the study.

There are reasons other than orthographic consistency which make languages easier or harder to learn. One of these is the number of symbols in the writing system: the European languages have fewer than 35 while others have as many as 2,500. For readers of languages with extensive symbolic systems like Chinese, which has more than 2,000 characters, learning can be expected to continue through the middle and high school years. The visual–spatial complexity of the symbols may add further to the burden of learning as has been observed in some of the Southern Indian languages. Furthermore, some writing systems embody diacritical markers that are important for pronunciation or for distinguishing homophones. In syllabaries, such as the Japanese hiragana, mappings are between symbols and syllables, but the challenge for the beginning reader is complicated because the language also comprises a more abstract orthographic system. This system, kanji, originally based on Chinese characters, also needs to be mastered and is further complicated by having both

Chinese and Japanese readings for each character depending on context. Figure 6 illustrates the relationship between the number of symbols (the orthographic breadth) and the visual complexity within the symbols in some of the world's writing systems; when there are more symbols in a writing system, the learning demands increase. Unsurprisingly, visual–orthographic difficulties have been reported in poor readers who are learning in extensive orthographies.

Languages also differ importantly in the ways they represent phonology and meaning. Chinese, often referred to as a morphographic language, represents perhaps the starkest contrast with English. Chinese characters often represent meaningful units of the language (the morphemes) though they may also represent abstract ideas. They also contain features called phonetic radicals which provide clues to the sounds that the symbols represent (but not systematically as in an alphabetic language or

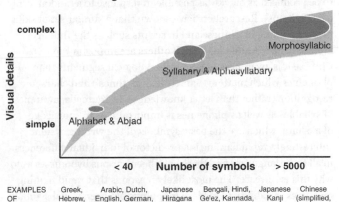

Learning demands differ across writing systems

complex						Morphosyllabic
				Syllabary & Alphasyllabary		
Visual details						
simple	Alphabet & Abjad					
	< 40	**Number of symbols**				> 5000

EXAMPLES OF LANGUAGES:	Greek, Hebrew, Italian	Arabic, Dutch, English, German, Kiswahili, Malay, Norwegian, Russian	Japanese Hiragana	Bengali, Hindi, Ge'ez, Kannada, Nepali, Punjabi, Thai, Sinhala	Japanese Kanji	Chinese (simplified, traditional)

6. Figure illustrating two dimensions of the world's writing systems: the number of symbols (the orthographic breadth) and the visual complexity within the symbols.

syllabary). It is not surprising, therefore, that the skills involved in learning Chinese differ from those involved in learning English. The most obvious differences relate to the phonological and semantic structures that need to be learned. Learning to read Chinese demands phonological awareness of the pitch of syllables (or 'tones'). It also demands awareness of the morphological structure of the language (how words are formed of compounds which combine lexical and meaning-based information); this is much less relevant for English.

Different demands but similar requirements?

Given the many differences between languages and writing systems, there is remarkable similarity between the predictors of individual differences in reading across languages. The ELDEL study showed that for children reading alphabetic languages there are three significant predictors of growth in reading in the early years of schooling. These are letter knowledge, phoneme awareness, and rapid naming (a test in which the names of colours or objects have to be produced as quickly as possible in response to a random array of such items). Researchers have shown that a similar set of skills predict reading in Chinese and in scripts such as the Indian alphasyllabary Kannada, though others are important too. In Chinese it is awareness of larger phonological segments than phonemes which matters (namely lexical 'tones') and character recognition (rather than letter knowledge). In Kannada, awareness of syllables as well as phonemes is important, as is knowledge of akshara, which are the basic symbols of the writing system. Interestingly, rapid naming is a predictor of individual differences in all these languages and there have been various hypotheses as to why this is the case. The most likely reason is that rapid naming measures the ability to retrieve mappings between visual symbols and verbal labels and is therefore a proxy for reading itself.

In summary, a 'triple foundation' of symbol knowledge, phonological awareness, and rapid naming ability appears to underpin reading development universally. However, there are also additional predictors that are language-specific. For Chinese, another critical predictor is awareness of the morphological structure of words. In addition, visual memory and visuo-spatial skills are stronger predictors of learning to read in a visually complex writing system, such as Chinese or Kannada, than they are for English. Moreover, there is emerging evidence of reciprocal relations—that learning to read in a complex orthography hones visuo-spatial abilities just as phoneme awareness improves as English children learn to read.

Dyslexia as a written language disorder

Children differ in the rate at which they learn to read and spell and children with dyslexia are typically the slowest to do so, assuming standard instruction for all. Indeed, it is clear from the outset that they have more difficulty in learning letters (by name or by sound) than their peers. As we have seen, letter knowledge is a crucial component of alphabetic competence and also offers a way into spelling. So for the dyslexic child with poor letter knowledge, learning to read and spell is compromised from the outset. In addition, there is a great deal of evidence that children with dyslexia have problems with phonological aspects of language from an early age and specifically, acquiring phonological awareness. This was true of Bobby (and possibly Harry too because, as an adult, he still scores poorly on tests of phoneme awareness and the odd speech error can be heard in his speech). The result is usually a significant problem in decoding—in fact, poor decoding is the hallmark of dyslexia, the signature of which is a nonword reading deficit. In the absence of remediation, this decoding difficulty persists and for many reading becomes something to be avoided. Some more fortunate individuals can nevertheless develop a reasonable sight vocabulary. Indeed, the most common pattern of reading deficit in dyslexia is an inability to read 'new' or unfamiliar words in the face of better developed word-reading skills—sometimes referred to as 'phonological dyslexia'.

The profile of phonological reading impairment is not, however, found in all dyslexic readers. Some who compensate well (Misha is a good example) are less severely impaired in reading nonwords than in reading so called 'exception' or irregular words; they may be confused about homophones, such as *leek* and *leak*, because they rely too heavily on phonological recoding and are not able to make reference to high-quality orthographic representations. The term 'surface dyslexia' (borrowed from the literature on dyslexia following brain injury) has sometimes been used to describe these individuals. While their phonological awareness is better developed than that of children with phonological dyslexia, they are not always free of such difficulties and they may have problems with the development of reading fluency, putting them at risk of knock-on effects on reading comprehension.

Spelling poses a significant challenge to children with dyslexia. This seems inevitable, given their problems with phoneme awareness and decoding. The early spelling attempts of children with dyslexia are typically not phonetic in the way that their peers' attempts are; rather, they are often difficult to decipher and best described as bizarre. In severe cases, difficulties with the phonological sequences of spellings persist, as in AVENTER for '*adventure*'. The persistence of phonological problems can be seen reflected in the spellings of a boy with severe dyslexia, studied from age 8. As the samples of his writing in Figure 7 show, his errors continue to reflect profound difficulties in representing the sounds of words as well as their conventional forms even at 12 and 16 years of age. Although not as severely affected as JM, most people with dyslexia continue to show poor spelling through development and there is a very high correlation between (poor) spelling in the teenage years and (poor) spelling in middle age. This in turn appears to have an impact on the development of writing and composition, though the precise mechanisms are not known.

Few adults with dyslexia read for pleasure. But this is not to imply that dyslexia is associated with problems in reading for meaning.

London

Loddon is the catoval and England in the steet there are lot of Black Taxi and larger biling The Queen living in london and the steet are aratd with people lot of train come in and out of London Hawod is in london to and it verg atfpensif

J.M. Age 12 years

A ampbilbians are arimals which live in water and Land a frog is one ampbilbians laht it egg in water tuzer are amphibican too. some can been very big. Some can be small.

J.M. 14·3·85

7. Writing samples from case JM at ages 12 and 16 years showing many dysphonetic errors.

While poor decoding can be a barrier to reading comprehension, many children and adults with dyslexia can read with adequate understanding when this is required but it takes them considerable time to do so, and they tend to avoid writing when it is possible to do so.

Chapter 3
What are the cognitive causes of dyslexia?

Before we begin to think about why some people can't read fluently, it is important to emphasize that there are different 'levels' of explanation for the causes of a specific learning disorder such as dyslexia. First, it is important to separate biological causes which are constitutional from environmental causes which impinge upon the individual during development (including in the period before birth). Although this distinction is not clear cut—genes act through the environment and environmental influences can also affect gene expression (referred to as 'epigenetics')—it is useful to keep them separate. Second, it is important to recognize that the defining feature of dyslexia—poor reading—is a behaviour and that this behaviour depends upon a range of cognitive abilities. A key challenge for the field of dyslexia is to understand its cognitive or 'proximal' causes. Furthermore, a causal theory at the cognitive level of explanation provides the rationale for the design of interventions which can moderate dyslexia's impact. Ultimately a complete causal theory would seek to understand how the biological make-up of individuals like Bobby, Misha, and Harry has affected brain development, and in turn compromised the cognitive processes that underlie the ability to learn to read.

Seeking causal evidence is not, however, straightforward. Cause is not the same as correlation. Correlation—the association of two events or two measures—is the first step to understanding a cause.

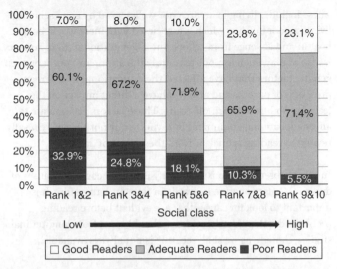

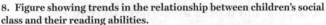

8. Figure showing trends in the relationship between children's social class and their reading abilities.

Causes operate at different levels and may be more distant (distal) or closer (proximal) to the outcome. There is, for example, a significant association between children's social class and their reading skills. This is shown in Figure 8 which displays data from a representative sample of 672 high school children in the UK tested during the standardization of the *York Assessment of Reading and Comprehension*; it can be seen that there are fewer good readers and more poor readers among those with the highest level of social deprivation. But is this association causal?

It can be seen from the figure that, while 32.9 per cent of children in the lowest social class are poor readers, some 7 per cent are good readers. Similarly, 5.5 per cent of children of the highest social class are poor readers. Surely, then, social class cannot be a cause of poor reading; if it is, then there are a lot of intervening variables. Social disadvantage is associated with a number of adverse factors which affect educational opportunity.

These include: living in an area not well-served by good schools; living in poor housing which is associated with increases in poor health; and absence from school. Inter-generational disadvantage is also at play, such as poor parental education, and perhaps even genetic factors that have affected the educational and career prospects of parents and also will have a direct impact on the learning abilities of their offspring. These factors accumulate to affect educational attainment but whether or not they are causally related to reading is unclear from these sorts of data.

In this chapter, the aim is to identify proximal cognitive causes of dyslexia. Causes operate forwards in time and, therefore, it is important to look for causes that are evident before reading problems develop. Ideally, evidence should come from longitudinal studies, though, as we shall see, this is not always available.

Individual differences in learning to read

We can get clues as to the causes of dyslexia by examining what predicts individual difference in reading skills among typically developing children. Since there is no absolute cut-off between dyslexia and 'normal' reading, what causes variation in reading in the population at large provides important evidence. We have already discussed two skills that are particularly important for decoding: phoneme awareness and letter knowledge. Together these predict how quickly reading accuracy develops in English readers between the ages of 4 and 6 years. Word reading is also associated with other phonological skills such as verbal short-term memory and rapid naming, the ability to retrieve the names of familiar colours, objects, or digits in a speeded naming task. In particular, data from a three-year longitudinal study of Norwegian children show that rapid naming (RAN) of symbols predicts growth in reading fluency beyond the early stages of learning to read.

What is known about dyslexia makes sense in relation to what is known about typical reading development. We have seen that children with dyslexia are slow to learn letters and also to develop phoneme awareness; it follows that the outcome for them is poor decoding. They also show deficits in RAN which compromise the rate at which they can read. Poor decoding fluency and relatedly a low level of reading accuracy is a 'bottleneck' to reading comprehension. However, when vocabulary and language understanding are good, individuals with dyslexia can sometimes compensate for poor decoding by drawing on these skills. Misha appears to have been doing this, using, for example, sentence context and employing high-level inferencing skills to help her to decipher print and to facilitate decoding—as we saw in Chapter 2, a process sometimes known as 'bootstrapping'.

Can we predict how well children will learn to read from the preschool years?

Although research on the predictors of reading at school age gets us a long way towards understanding the risk signs for dyslexia at school, a key question remains: can we identify the predictors of dyslexia from an even earlier stage in development, long before reading instruction begins? Relatively few studies have addressed this question but evidence shows that preschool spoken language skills, including the size of a child's vocabulary, the way in which they can put words together in sentences, and measures such as their ability to use grammar to signal past tense, are strong predictors of the development of phoneme awareness. This reinforces the view that oral language sets the stage for literacy development.

A recent longitudinal study of English children, many of whom were at risk of dyslexia, showed that language skills measured at age 3½ predict reading accuracy at 5½ years. Moreover, their impact on the development of decoding is via phoneme awareness and letter knowledge at age 4½ as depicted in Figure 9. In this study, language also predicted RAN at 4½ but did not influence reading a year later at age 5½; in English, the influence of RAN is

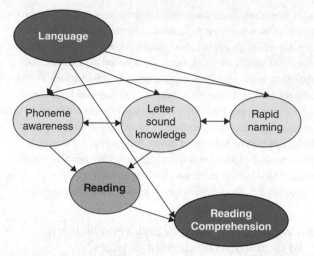

9. **Model of predictive relationships showing how oral language is the foundation of reading development and causally related to reading comprehension via phoneme awareness and letter sound skills.**

not apparent until reading develops beyond the early stage and fluency can be measured. A further important finding of this study was that early spoken language skills predict how good a child's reading comprehension is some five years later at age 8–9 years—a finding that highlights a remarkably robust long-range effect of spoken language skills on literacy development.

The verbal deficit hypothesis

Since children with dyslexia have normal vision but cannot remember the visual forms of words (as was the case with Misha), a natural hypothesis is that dyslexia is caused by some kind of 'visual perceptual' deficit. Indeed, for many years, psychologists were intrigued by the preponderance of reversals and ordering errors in the reading and writing of children with dyslexia, for example, confusing '*b*' with '*d*' or reading '*was*' as '*saw*'. However, it turned out that these problems were not specifically visual in origin. Rather, children with dyslexia are as prone to confuse letters which sounded similar, such as 'k' and 'g', as they are to confuse letters which looked similar. Perhaps more significant was the work of Frank Vellutino in New Jersey, who reported a series of studies which provided strong evidence against the visual deficit hypothesis. In one of these studies, he asked poor readers to remember letter strings taken either from the English or from the Hebrew alphabet and compared their performance with that of children without reading difficulties. While the poor readers were impaired when reproducing the English letter strings, they performed at the same level as controls when reproducing the Hebrew ones (with which neither group were familiar). Drawing together this evidence with other empirical data available at the time, Vellutino went on to recast the visual deficit hypothesis as consistent with a verbal coding deficit. In short, verbal memory deficits could account for many of the phenomena associated with dyslexia. A similar conclusion was drawn from a study in the UK; this showed that while children with dyslexia could recall sequences of abstract shapes as well as controls (indicating their visual memory was 'normal'), they had significant difficulty in remembering sequences of letters. Interestingly the ability of the poor readers to recall the letter sequences improved significantly when they were allowed to trace over the letters first. In contrast, normal readers did not derive this benefit; they did not need to use a compensatory code because their verbal memory was intact.

Refining the verbal deficit hypothesis

The verbal deficit hypothesis marked a turning point in research on dyslexia and chimed with data from population studies which had shown that children with specific reading difficulties often have a history of speech and language difficulties. But the hypothesis that dyslexia was caused by language difficulties which compromised verbal coding was too broad. Language is a complex system within which different subsystems interact in the process of comprehending and producing language. The semantic system is concerned with word meaning, the grammatical system with how words are put together in phrases, and the phonological system with how speech sounds signal changes in meaning (e.g. the words '*bit*' and '*pit*' differ by a single phoneme but they mean different things). In addition, the pragmatic system is concerned with how words are used to communicate. It was always clear that not all of these systems are impaired in dyslexia; after all, many people with dyslexia have good knowledge of the meanings of words (vocabulary) and some are excellent communicators. On the other hand, their problems with phoneme awareness already give a clue that phonological skills are impaired and, perhaps to a lesser extent grammatical skills, since phonological cues often signal differences in grammar (e.g. the difference between the present tense 'love' and the past tense 'loved' is carried by the change of a single phoneme). Therefore, should the verbal deficit hypothesis be recast as the phonological deficit hypothesis?

The origins of the phonological deficit hypothesis of dyslexia can be traced to work by the Haskins group, who observed that beginning readers find it difficult to segment the phonemes in spoken words. It was only a short step from this observation to their discovery of a range of phonological deficits in dyslexia, including striking deficits in phonological memory. In a classic experiment, they compared the performance of good and poor readers in tasks tapping memory for strings of letters with phonologically confusable names, like GPVTB, and non-confusable strings, like HWTRS. Good readers could remember fewer of the items from confusable than from non-confusable strings. This observation indicated that they were automatically recoding the letters into their phonemic counterparts and hence confusing them in the former case. In contrast, the poor readers were not subject to this 'phonetic confusability effect'. Although this finding has since been criticized on methodological grounds (because the two groups were not equated for memory on the non-confusable strings), it was a landmark finding which highlighted the nature of the dyslexic problem. Subsequent replications using better methods have essentially replicated the results; in fact, poor verbal short-term memory for digits (which are best coded phonologically) is a hallmark of dyslexia.

In the 1970s I was conducting research at the Dyslexia Clinic at St Bartholomew's Hospital in London. There I noticed that children with dyslexia had two problems which seemed to fit with those reported by the Haskins group: the first a problem with 'word attack' skills which persisted despite an improvement in word-reading skill and second, a problem in pronouncing complex multisyllabic words. Similar problems had been noted by Tim Miles, who set up the Dyslexia Unit in Bangor, North Wales. These observations led me to conduct experiments on nonword reading and nonword repetition in dyslexia, comparing each in turn with the same processes but using known lexical items (words).

The tasks used were simple: they required participants to read nonwords, like *'tegwop'*, or to repeat long items, like *'basquetty'*. The children with dyslexia made more errors even on these apparently simple tasks than expected given their ability to read and repeat real words; and, importantly, difficulties were apparent not only in relation to their age but in relation to younger children reading at the same level. This finding suggested that something was affecting their ability to segment words into phonemes—something required both for establishing a new articulation programme for pronouncing new words and for establishing the mappings between phonemes and graphemes required for the decoding of nonwords. It seemed that the children with dyslexia were able to read words lexically if their visual forms had been committed to memory but had problems with new forms. Similarly, they could repeat familiar words when they were committed to lexical memory but had trouble when a new word had to be learned. While the theoretical interpretation of these findings has been refined over time, phonological problems within this domain are characteristic features of dyslexia across the age range.

The phonological deficit hypothesis

We have now discussed several of the areas in which children (and adults) with dyslexia show significant difficulty: phonological awareness, verbal short-term memory, slowness in naming (in RAN tasks), and difficulty in repeating nonsense words they have not heard before (e.g. *'blonterstaping'*). They also can experience marked difficulties in finding the right word to say and problems in learning new names for objects or for symbols. Together, these problems cause considerable difficulty in educational settings. Imagine what it must be like to try to learn a foreign language if you have difficulty in repeating new words and learning new names, and, even if you know a word or someone's name well, a problem bringing it to mind (see Figure 10). Interestingly, some adults with dyslexia who have learned to read to an adequate level of proficiency complain more about their memory problems than their poor literacy.

Phonological deficits are widely believed to be the root cause of dyslexia. However, one of the problems to be faced when assessing the *causal* status of these deficits is that performance on phonological tasks is influenced by reading skill. Two examples illustrate this point. In an elegant demonstration of the influence of learning to read on phoneme awareness, it has been shown that readers think there is a [t] sound in the spoken word *'pitch'* but not in the word *'rich'*, revealing a strong influence of orthographic experience. A rather different example comes from adult illiterates studied by Castro-Caldas and colleagues using brain imagery. In this study, literate women and their poorly educated (and hence illiterate) sisters were asked to repeat words and nonwords while brain activity was measured. The literate women activated different brain regions when repeating words from those they activated when repeating nonwords. In contrast, their illiterate sisters showed brain activation only in regions of the brain that serve the semantic processing of words. The implication of these findings is

'One of the worst things about dyslexia
is when you have something important to say
but can't find the ?!.......!?'

10. Word-finding difficulties, common in dyslexia.

that there are brain changes associated with learning to read in
the systems that underpin phonological processing (and these are
activated when novel word forms are presented). It follows that
deficits in phonological processes in dyslexia could be a consequence
rather than a cause of poor reading. While studies demonstrating
that children at high risk of dyslexia show phonological
impairments well before they begin formal literacy instruction
refute this possibility, it remains an issue for some researchers.

43

There are also refinements of the phonological deficit theory to be considered. One of these proposes a distinction between dyslexic readers whose problems are associated with poor phoneme awareness and dyslexic readers whose main problem is with rapid naming and still others who have a 'double-deficit'. Other theories, as we shall see, implicate impairments in sensory systems that pre-date phonological deficits.

Auditory and speech processing in dyslexia: a cascade of deficits?

A number of theories of dyslexia try to explain how basic sensory or perceptual problems could lead to phonological deficits. The most influential of these proposes that dyslexia is due to a problem with the rapid temporal processing of incoming auditory information which, in turn, is needed for the perception of speech sounds. Within this framework a cascade of difficulty from auditory processing through speech perception compromises the development of phonological representations in dyslexia and thereby accounts for both phonological deficits and, later, a problem in mapping between graphemes and phonemes (see Figure 11).

A large number of studies have tested aspects of this 'cascade' theory, many using a rapid auditory processing (RAP) task though few provide longitudinal data. In the RAP task, children listen to a pair of tones varying in pitch (high versus low). In the first part of the experiment, they learn to associate a high

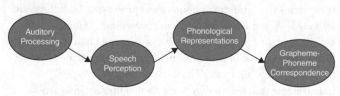

11. How auditory perception might influence learning to read: a 'cascade' model.

tone with an upward-pointing arrow and a low tone with a downward-pointing arrow. Once they have learned the associations, the next task is for them to listen to a pair of tones and to reproduce the sequence (high–low, low–high, high–high, or low–low). An additional feature of the experiment is that the tones in the sequences are separated by variable time intervals; sometimes the tones are presented close in time, sometimes with a longer gap between them.

Children with dyslexia struggle with the RAP task and make many errors. What is unclear is whether a problem revealed by this task is in the *temporal* processing or in the *rapid* processing of auditory information. There is another problem too. It is common to use some form of verbal labelling when completing the task (saying '*high*' or '*low*' under your breath) so, the fact that children with dyslexia have verbal deficits might mean they have difficulties with the task because their coding strategies are inefficient.

More recent research pursuing the auditory deficit hypothesis has focused on temporal processing, using tasks such as perceiving a 'gap' in a tone, and also on a range of other perceptual skills relevant to speech perception. These include measures of sensitivity to pitch, intensity, sound modulation (variations in pitch or loudness), stimulus onset and duration. Many studies have reported differences in performance between groups of dyslexic readers and controls; others report moderate correlations between auditory processing and reading skill. However, most studies have involved older children or adults and longitudinal studies are rare. It is clear that if a basic auditory processing problem sets the stage for a cascade of difficulties leading to poor reading, then such difficulties should be apparent early in development and be predictive of later speech perception and phoneme awareness. A recent study from our Wellcome Language and Reading Project tested this hypothesis by examining the predictive relationships between a measure of auditory processing requiring the discrimination of tones differing in frequency (or pitch) in children at risk of dyslexia and controls. We first measured frequency discrimination at age 4½ and investigated how well it predicted language and reading a year later and reading at age 8 years. We found no evidence that frequency discrimination predicted either reading or language. Rather, we found a strong correlation between children's performance in the frequency discrimination task and their language and attentional skills, and it was language which predicted reading. Furthermore, it was children with poor language (and also poor attention) who had most difficulty in frequency discrimination and not children at family risk of dyslexia. This suggests that problems on such tasks reflect poor attention and do not have any direct association with dyslexia.

Researchers have also attributed poor phonological skills in dyslexia to problems with speech perception. The typical task used to assess speech perception involves asking people to discriminate between, or identify, pairs of similar-sounding phonemes, such as 'bee' [bi]–'pea' [pi]. The speech stimuli used are synthesized in such a way that they vary along a continuum according to a critical feature, such as the timing between different spectral components. The striking thing is, however, that although the stimuli vary continuously on a given acoustic dimension they are perceived either as sounding like 'pea' or sounding like 'bee' and never a mix of the two. This is referred to as categorical perception—we hear 'bee' or 'pea' but never something that sounds like a mixture of the two phonemes /p/ and /b/. People with dyslexia are less accurate on tasks like this. They have particular difficulty around the acoustic boundary between the two sounds, suggesting they have difficulty in categorizing the sounds as phonemes.

Many studies have reported deficits in speech perception in groups of children and adults with dyslexia. However, more recent findings suggest that not all children with reading difficulties have speech perception problems. Rather, it is children who have co-occurring oral language difficulties who are the most likely to do poorly on such tasks. Furthermore, many children with dyslexia have problems in sustaining attention; the fact that laboratory-based speech perception tasks are long and highly demanding of attention provides another plausible reason for the poor performance of children with dyslexia.

A neat way of assessing individual differences in what is described as 'categorical speech perception' is to compare the performance of children with dyslexia, children with oral language difficulties (developmental language disorder), and children with both conditions. In addition, by embedding clear speech tokens which are easy to perceive among the harder items, it is possible to monitor attention as the task proceeds. Using strategies such as these, our Wellcome Language and Reading Project found evidence for both propositions. First, children with poor reading accompanied by poor language have speech perception problems, whereas those with purely dyslexic difficulties are much less likely to have such problems. Second, children with difficulties in the executive control of attention are particularly likely to fail—and their performance across trials is highly variable.

One way around the problem of poor attention is to investigate the causes of dyslexia using physiological measures of the brain's response to speech sounds. Studies have produced some evidence for a lack of sensitivity to speech–sound differences in dyslexia, including in infants at family risk of dyslexia; but findings are mixed. According to Usha Goswami, the speech perceptual problem may be at a higher level than the individual speech sound. This hypothesis proposes a difficulty in extracting prosodic structure from speech as a cause of later emerging language and phonological difficulties. However, as yet, longitudinal data are lacking.

Visual theories of dyslexia

Given that reading requires establishing mappings between language and vision, some theorists have suggested a possible causal connection between visual processing impairments and dyslexia. Rather than being a resurgence of old ideas about visual memory deficits in dyslexia, the deficits implicated are in processes such as the perception of contrast and motion and in eye movement control. Bill Lovegrove, a visual psychophysicist, was the first to propose this idea in 1984. In order to understand the hypothesis, it is necessary to provide a thumbnail sketch of the visual system.

In simple terms, visual information received through the retina at the back of each eye is transferred to the visual cortex of the brain. These signals from the eyes are processed via a 'magnocellular system' (specialized for fast-moving, brief stimuli of low spatial frequency) and a 'parvocellular system' (specialized for processing static or slow-moving stimuli of high spatial frequency or colour). In turn, information is passed on through an area called the lateral geniculate nucleus (LGN) to the cortex either via the upper (dorsal) stream (a continuation of the magnocellular system) or the lower (ventral) stream of visual cortex which extends the parvocellular system (see Figure 12). The dorsal stream, particularly

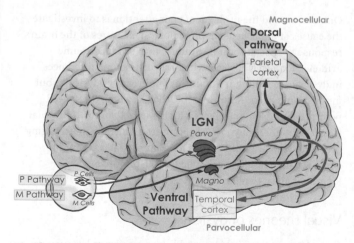

12. The magnocellular ('where') and parvocellular ('what') pathways from the retina to the visual cortex of the brain.

the region called V5/MT, is primarily responsible for the perception of motion and for the control of eye movements (though it also receives input from the other stream).

Much work on visual aspects of dyslexia has focused on tasks thought to depend on one or other of the two visual processing systems (the magnocellular and parvocellular systems). Essentially, participants in these experiments view two visual displays and have to say, for example, whether the dots on the screen are moving to the left or to the right. The experiment manipulates the displays systematically (in this example, many of the dots are moving randomly in different directions on the screen and the experimenter varies the proportion of dots moving in the same direction). The ability to detect the direction of movement in such a display reflects the magnocellular system. According to Lovegrove, dyslexia is associated with problems of the magnocellular visual system revealed by tasks such as this. The theory was bolstered by findings of reduced brain activity in the V5/MT area during visual motion-processing in dyslexia, as well as findings that cells in the magnocellular layers of LGN are smaller in people with dyslexia than in typical readers.

However, the theory of magnocellular deficits in dyslexia has been challenged on a number of grounds. Most critically, the theory fails to explain how a problem in seeing moving stimuli viewed in conditions of low luminosity could be a cause of reading difficulties (not least because reading usually takes place in good light conditions with stationary text). The correlation between sensitivity of the magnocellular system/dorsal stream and reading is relatively weak and it has been argued that such effects are unlikely to reflect a cause of the reading problems in dyslexia.

One recent study seems particularly useful in resolving inconsistencies in the evidence regarding low-level visual deficits. The study falls into three parts. First, using measures of brain activation, the study replicated the classic finding of reduced activity in the region of V5/MT during visual motion-processing in dyslexia. Second, measures of brain activation in this region showed no differences between normal readers and younger children with dyslexia, matched in reading level and performance IQ. This 'null effect' suggests that the lack of activation in V5/MT might relate to reading experience rather than providing a causal explanation for dyslexia. If true, then any improvement in reading brought about by intervention should be accompanied by increased brain activation. Third, the study found there was an increase in brain activity in V5/MT after a period of intervention which had led to an improvement in reading skills. Although a weakness of this study is that control data are not provided, the findings are interesting and cast doubt on the hypothesis that dyslexia is the consequence of low-level visual impairments.

Visual attention

A further version of a 'visual' theory of dyslexia suggests that individuals with dyslexia have difficulty in directing visual attention and offers a possible explanation for why some children with dyslexia show orthographic rather than phonological deficits (it will be recalled that Misha had only mild phonological deficits but her orthographic skills were poor as judged by her spelling).

According to the visual attention theory of dyslexia, poor visual attention span can affect the left-to-right extraction of letter-based information from print. Since this is critical for dividing up letter strings prior to the application of decoding rules, it would ultimately affect the development of the orthographic system. In a test of the visual attention theory, children are asked to view a display of letters presented simultaneously for a short period. Next, they are asked to report one of two things: either they should report all of the letters in the display or, if they see an arrow, they should report the letter which had appeared at the position in the string where the arrow is pointing. In the latter 'partial report' condition, the typical child can report the letter which was in the centre of the string more accurately than those to the left or right (they do rather better at the end points). Children with dyslexia are significantly less accurate than controls when the letter to be reported is in the periphery, suggesting that their visual attention span is smaller than that of a typical reader.

However, since we know that children with dyslexia are slower to name letters than typical readers, it could be that what causes the problem is slow initial coding of the letters rather than any limitation in visual attention. In a neat demonstration of this, researchers adapted the visual attention task to remove the need to name the letters, replacing this element with a task in which, at each serial position, the correct item and an alternative were presented so that the child just had to make a choice. They then compared the performance of dyslexic and non-dyslexic readers for letter strings, for strings of digits, and crucially also for strings of non-nameable symbols. The results in Figure 13 show that the children with dyslexia had reduced visual attention for letter strings and also for strings of digits yet their span for non-nameable symbols was normal. It seems from this experiment that the dyslexic problem is principally to do with the verbal coding of

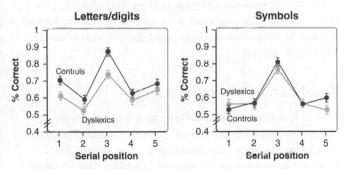

13. Figure showing accuracy of recalling stimuli presented to the left and right of the focus of attention for letters and digits (left panel) and for non-alphanumeric symbols (right panel). The dyslexia deficit is only in processing letters and digits.

letters and digits and not specifically a consequence of limited visual attention span. In short, these data refute the visual attention theory as a causal hypothesis of dyslexia.

Visual stress

It has also been proposed that, while not a specific cause of dyslexia, visual discomfort (or stress) can affect reading, particularly reading fluency. Visual stress, sometimes referred to as Meares/Irlen syndrome, is associated with the experience of perceptual distortions, such as letters moving around the page. This can make reading aversive. Proponents of the visual stress theory advocate the use of coloured lenses or filters placed over print to reduce glare. In turn, this simple procedure is said to lead to increased reading speed and better reading comprehension.

The views of the ophthalmic profession are divided as to both the 'diagnosis' of visual stress and the efficacy of its treatments. More generally, the association between visual symptoms and poor reading is doubtful. A recent study using data from the large cohort of children aged 7–9 years participating in the *Avon Longitudinal Study of Parents and Children* found little evidence of an association between severe reading difficulties and the kinds of visual difficulties which are commonly seen in children referred to eye clinics because of problems with vision (such as lazy eye and myopia).

Broader impairments in dyslexia

Beyond visual and auditory theories of dyslexia, a number of theories propose that the causes of dyslexia can be found in systems which compromise learning in rather general ways. Proposed deficits include an inability to adopt a stable point of reference in perceptual tasks ('anchoring') and problems in implicit learning or in developing automatic (non-conscious) control of motor skills. To take one example, the cerebellar deficit hypothesis suggests that children with dyslexia can learn new skills but cannot automatize them. One of the tasks they used to confirm this theory involved asking children to learn a finger and thumb sequencing task; once they had learned it, they had to perform it fluently several times. Children with dyslexia had more difficulty learning the task and were much slower in the test trials than were normal readers.

A second task involved asking children to balance on a beam, one leg at a time with their eyes closed. Once this had been accomplished, children were required to continue to balance while counting backwards in threes. Children with dyslexia were much more likely to wobble or even fall off the beam than controls in this task, suggesting that, for them, balance required conscious control. However, an illuminating review later showed that when problems of balance in dyslexia are observed, these appear to be associated with co-occurring disorders, such as ADHD, and are not due to dyslexia per se. More generally, even if some children with dyslexia have difficulties in motor learning and coordination, such problems do not have the potential to explain their difficulties in learning to read (and spell) or their failure to develop fluent reading.

In summary, it is difficult to see how theories implicating broad deficits in dyslexia could explain the specificity of the learning disorder which is observed. If learning were to be compromised in rather general ways, much wider-spread problems than those seen in dyslexia would be likely to ensue.

Can we agree on what causes dyslexia?

We have seen that there are a number of different cognitive theories concerning the causes of dyslexia. Moreover, the range of causal deficits that have been proposed has led some people to suggest that we dismiss the concept of 'dyslexia' as having little utility. After more than fifty years of scientific research, this would be to throw out the proverbial baby with the bath water. A critical review shows that there is more consensus than the sceptics imply. What is needed is a conceptual framework which can draw together converging evidence from a variety of methodologies to elucidate the development of dyslexia. The evidence should straddle investigations of dyslexia as a dimensional disorder (approaches which correlate cognitive skills with reading abilities) and those which use case-control methods to investigate dyslexia as though it were a diagnostic 'category'. In addition, the framework should incorporate evidence from training studies which can test causal theories.

To prepare the way, two further sets of studies need to be considered. First, we need to consider whether individuals might differ relative to one another as well as in the cognitive deficits associated with dyslexia. After all, it would be surprising if our three cases, Bobby, Misha, and Harry, did not have different strengths and weaknesses. Second, we need to invoke the concept of 'causal precedence' and seek evidence of the precursors of dyslexia at an early stage in development before literacy begins to shape the cognitive system.

Pursuing the first approach, Franck Ramus and his colleagues took the important step, not of pitting one theory against another, but of investigating the numbers of individuals within a sample of people with dyslexia who experience the various deficits that have been proposed. In the first of these studies of children, assessments were made of phonological skills, auditory processing, visual motion detection, visual stress, and motor skills. Using typical readers as a control group, a deficit was defined as falling one standard deviation below the mean of the control group. Of 23 children with dyslexia, 12 showed phonological deficits, 6 auditory deficits, 2 visual motion deficits, 8 visual stress, and 5 motor deficits. The findings confirmed, as expected, that only a minority of children with dyslexia have sensory or motor impairments. The phonological deficit was the most common deficit to be observed (though not all individuals were affected) and phonological tasks were the only kinds of task on which differences between good and poor readers were significant.

A replication of this approach with a much larger sample of 164 French children with dyslexia (of greater severity than in the previous study) examined performance on tasks tapping phonological skills, visual stress, and visual attention span. Once again, phonological deficits were the most widespread: over 90 per cent of the sample showed these deficits. In contrast, the percentage of children experiencing visual stress was 5.5 per cent, no more than for controls. The findings for visual attention span were interesting. Some 28 per cent of the children with dyslexia showed reduced attention span; however, all of these also experienced phonological deficits, refuting the argument that deficits in visual attention account for reading difficulties in children who do not experience phonological deficits.

The findings of these case series (and others) provide some compelling evidence for the phonological deficit hypothesis. However, not every person with dyslexia has a phonological deficit—at least not at the point when they are assessed—and others may be only mildly impaired; still others may have poor phonological skills because learning to read has not refined their phonological representations. This is why studies involving the assessment of cognitive skills before reading fails to develop are important.

Children at family risk of dyslexia

Some of the strongest evidence for the developmental profile of dyslexia comes from longitudinal studies of children who have a first-degree relative with dyslexia (usually a parent and sometimes a sibling). These have been conducted in children from different language backgrounds including English, Dutch, Finnish, Czech, Slovak, and Chinese. They have followed children at family risk of dyslexia from preschool through the early school years, with two studies starting when the children were infants. According to a systematic review of the published studies, the probability of becoming dyslexic if you are at family risk is, on average, 45 per cent, compared with 12 per cent for children from families with no history of reading impairment. Put another way, almost one in every two children born to a dyslexic parent seems to develop reading difficulties. Furthermore, children at family risk of dyslexia, regardless of whether they eventually receive a 'dyslexia diagnosis', have poorer reading and spelling than controls, confirming that dyslexia is a dimensional disorder without a clear cut-off.

Turning to the preschool cognitive impairments observed in children with a dyslexic outcome, the review found, across studies, that phonological deficits were apparent from the early years—these were observed on tasks of nonword repetition, verbal memory, phonological awareness, and rapid naming. Poor letter knowledge was also observed, consistent with expectation given that these skills comprise the *triple foundation* of reading. However, in contrast to the theory that children with dyslexia have a very specific phonological deficit, the children who went on to be classified as dyslexic also showed a range of language difficulties beyond phonology, including poor grammar and vocabulary. Furthermore, it is clear that the probability of being 'diagnosed' dyslexic is greater if the child has persistent spoken language difficulties at school entry. A further critical factor differentiating children at family risk who do and do not become dyslexic was performance on the rapid naming task; a child was more likely to become dyslexic if they showed RAN deficits, in line with the double deficit hypothesis of dyslexia.

The findings of family risk studies, particularly the association between family risk and poor language, led our group to embark upon the Wellcome Language and Reading Project in 2007. In this study, we followed the progress of two groups of children at high risk of dyslexia: children at family risk because they had an affected parent and children with preschool language impairment. We first saw the children aged 3½ and followed them until age 8, assessing them at annual intervals. The key question for the present discussion is whether we found evidence of phonological deficits pre-reading instruction in those who went on to be classified as dyslexic. We did: children who were classified as having dyslexia at age 8 had problems from age 3½ in phonological aspects of language (nonword repetition) and from 4½ years they showed deficits in phoneme awareness and RAN relative to typically developing controls. These deficits were more severe in children who also fulfilled criteria for developmental language disorder at age 8. However, for children with developmental language disorder who were not also dyslexic, phonological difficulties, though present at the outset, declined over time, such that they did not succumb to decoding deficits (reading comprehension was however affected).

We can conclude, therefore, that it is appropriate to consider the phonological deficit as a precursor to dyslexia, and, importantly, one that pre-dates reading instruction. However, rather than being regarded as deterministic, it should be conceptualized as a *causal risk factor* which increases the probability of being dyslexic. Indeed, there is strong indication that it is only when a phonological deficit combines with other difficulties that dyslexia is the outcome. In milder cases—when an individual experiences a unitary deficit—it is more likely that the child will show some, but not all, of the signs of dyslexia (perhaps poor spelling or a lack of reading fluency, as we saw in the case of Misha). Such a profile, often seen in teenagers who receive a late 'diagnosis' in higher education, has been referred to as 'compensated dyslexia'; perhaps a more appropriate term would be the 'broader phenotype' of dyslexia. Using this terminology captures the fact that the heritable risk of dyslexia (seen in affected family members) initially manifests itself as a phonological deficit. A phonological deficit affects the process of learning to read and to spell to differing extents, depending on the presence of other risk and protective factors. Indeed, as Bruce Pennington has argued cogently, the aetiology of a disorder such as dyslexia is multifactorial. One way of thinking about the various causal theories of dyslexia is as highlighting the risk factors that are associated with a dyslexic outcome. Within Pennington's framework each risk factor may exacerbate the impact of core phonological deficits which comprise reading and increase the probability of a dyslexia diagnosis but data are still needed to pin down this argument.

Chapter 4
Dyslexia genes and the environment—a class act?

Bobby, Misha, and Harry all have dyslexia and they all have phonological deficits. The phonological deficit is milder in Misha than in Bobby and Harry and she also seems to be better able to get around her difficulties. However, as we shall see, one thing that unites them is a family history of reading and language difficulties. It is reasonable to suspect, therefore, that in each of these cases, dyslexia reflects a genetic predisposition though its manifestation is different for all three. This might be because there are differences in the severity of the core deficit, or because there are differences in the resources they have for compensation, or because they have been dealt different hands when it comes to their environments, including their schooling. This chapter will consider the biological bases of dyslexia and ask: what is the evidence that dyslexia is heritable? We will then go on to consider the role of the environment as a possible moderator of genetic influences.

Is dyslexia heritable?

It has been known for many years, certainly since the early writings of Samuel T. Orton, that dyslexia runs in families. Like other neurodevelopmental disorders, dyslexia has an early onset in childhood, is persistent (although its impact may lessen over time), and is likely to be heritable. Let us return to our three cases.

Bobby's father is an engineer who does not regard himself as 'much of a reader', but he has followed a successful career in industry and Bobby's mother is an office administrator. It seems that there is a history of speech difficulties and dyslexia in his father's family but no such history on his mother's side. Misha is the third child in her family. Her two older sisters are doing well academically though neither is good at maths. Her mother's brother had reading problems at school but the causes of his difficulties were never 'diagnosed'. Harry has dyslexia on both sides of the family; although neither of his parents had problems with literacy or numeracy, an uncle was affected and both of his cousins.

The genetics of dyslexia is an important but complicated issue. As mentioned, the family aggregation of reading problems had been noted by clinicians during the first half of the 20th century, before the first formal investigation of them in the 1950s. However, since families share genes and also environments, how can we tell whether the cause (or causes) of dyslexia are genetic? As we will see, it is the study of twins which provides the best opportunity of disentangling the effects of genes from the effects of shared environments.

Twin studies capitalize on the comparison of identical (monozygotic, MZ) twins, who share 100 per cent of their segregating genes, with fraternal (dizygotic, DZ) twins, who on average share 50 per cent. Since both types of twins mostly share the same environment (at least up until the teenage years), it is typically assumed that if MZ twins are more similar to each other than DZ twins this must principally reflect the greater genetic similarity of MZ twins. It turns out that the probability that both twins will have dyslexia (the concordance rate) is higher for MZ twins (about 90 per cent) than for DZ twins (about 40 per cent).

As we have seen, however, dyslexia has no clear-cut boundaries. Rather it is a dimensional disorder (varying from mild to severe); dyslexia is simply the lower end of a continuum of reading skills.

A limitation of concordance studies is that they treat dyslexia as 'all or none'—you either have it or you do not. In contrast, other techniques in behaviour genetics take account of the continuous variation in reading (or any trait) to assess its heritability. Using statistical modelling, this approach provides estimates of how much of the variability in reading scores between individuals on a reading scale is due to shared genes and how much is due to shared environment. Figure 14 presents the essential features of this approach. The approach assumes that if one twin in a DZ pair gains a low score on a reading test (the one affected with dyslexia called the proband), the score of their co-twin is likely to move towards the average range, whereas this 'drift', known as 'regression to the mean', is much smaller (or negligible) in MZ twin pairs. In other words, the amount of 'drift' is an indicator of the genetic influence on that trait.

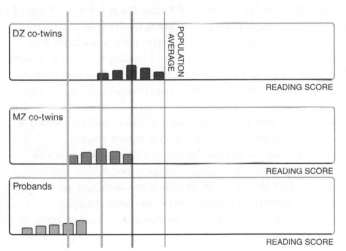

14. **Reading scores of probands with dyslexia (lower panel), MZ co-twins (middle panel), and DZ co-twins (upper panel). The score of the DZ co-twin moves further to the average of the population than does that of the MZ co-twin; known as 'regression to the mean'.**

Twin studies, provided they are large enough in scale, can be used to derive estimates of three sources of variability between individuals: the amount of variability in reading which is due to shared genes, the amount of variability due to shared environment, and the amount of variability due to what is referred to as non-shared environment (and includes the error associated with the measurement of the trait). 'Heritability' is an estimate of the amount of variability in a trait which is attributable to genetic variation; the higher the heritability, the more substantial the genetic contribution to that trait. Heritability estimates range from 0 (no genetic influence) to 1.0 (completely due to genes); heritability estimates for reading fluency are high, in the region of 0.7, meaning that 70 per cent of the variability in reading between people is attributable to genetic factors.

Much of the pioneering work investigating the genetic and environmental causes of reading and other learning disabilities emanates from the University of Colorado where the US National Institutes of Health have been funding the study of twins since 1992 and, more recently, The International Longitudinal Twin Study, a comparative study of children learning to read in Colorado, Australia, and Scandinavia. Findings of the studies confirm the genetic basis of individual differences in reading from the early years of schooling onwards. However, comparative data show that the environment has a greater influence before reading instruction begins, no doubt reflecting differences in home literacy environment and parental attitudes to literacy. There is also preliminary evidence that the learning processes involved in reading, including those involved in letter learning, have a somewhat different genetic basis to the language skills which are at the foundation of reading and, more so, reading comprehension.

Focusing on the low extreme of the reading skills distribution (dyslexia), these studies have provided indisputable evidence that group membership (being dyslexic) is largely due to shared genes.

They have also been used to assess the genetic contribution to the correlation between two traits. Two traits of particular interest are reading and one of its key foundations, phonological awareness. The important point here is that the genetic correlation between phonological awareness and reading, that is decoding, is high, suggesting common genetic influences and hence likely common causation of underlying mechanisms.

Behaviour genetic studies also make an important contribution to our understanding of the stability of reading skills over time. The large UK Twins Early Development Study (TEDS) has followed a cohort of twins from age 2 to young adulthood, measuring a wide range of traits including language, reading, and behaviour. This study is important because it can answer the question of whether the same influences (genetic and/or environmental) operate at different ages. Reading fluency was first measured at age 7 and subsequently at ages 12 and 16. The findings were clear: there are common genetic influences on reading at ages 7, 12, and 16 with further novel genetic influences coming into play at each of the later time points. In contrast, the effects of shared environment are small and in this study were only significant at age 7.

In the TEDS study, oral language was measured at the same ages as was reading. It was therefore possible to estimate the genetic correlation between language and reading. The correlation was moderate, suggesting that some 25 per cent of the same genetic influences are operating on language as on reading fluency (smaller than for phonological awareness). Interestingly, the genetic correlation between language and reading comprehension was much higher (over 0.8); this suggests that these two traits are closer in terms of the genes that affect them.

Overall, the findings of the TEDS project concur with those of the Colorado group and suggest, perhaps counterintuitively given that reading is a learned behaviour, that the effects of the environment on reading are relatively small. However, we must remember that the findings are specific to the samples studied and the range of environments they have experienced; and they capture some but not all of the genetic effects. Environmental effects can be expected to be stronger in an education system in which there is considerable variability between schools in the quality of education and in the curricula delivered. Further, the findings do not speak to the genetic and environmental causes of poor reading at the level of the individual child—they relate to group patterns. However even if we accept that there are strong genetic influences on our reading abilities this does not mean that interventions aimed at struggling readers cannot be effective.

Finding 'dyslexia genes'

Estimating how much of the variability in reading in a population is due to genetic influences takes us some way towards understanding heritability, but it does not help us to identify the genes associated with dyslexia. From the outset it is important to understand that there is no single gene for dyslexia; rather, genetic influences on dyslexia are likely to be due to many genes with small effects operating together. In the past two decades there has been enormous interest in the molecular genetics of dyslexia. While progress has been rapid, and so-called candidate genes have been identified, we expect that there will be thousands of genes involved so there are still large gaps in understanding. It is often said that we are 'a long way from accounting for the missing heritability'.

Before proceeding let us take a step back and rehearse what we know about how genes affect development. In each cell of the human body, there are twenty-three pairs of chromosomes (twenty-two pairs of autosomes and one pair of sex chromosomes). Chromosomes contain the hereditary material, or genes, from two parents and each person has two copies (or alleles) of each gene, one from their mother and one from their father. Genes are composed of sequences of DNA (deoxyribonucleic acid) and it is the sequences of DNA in the genes that carry what can be considered to be the 'instructions' for the development of the organism (see Figure 15). It is here, therefore, that the heritable differences between individuals originate.

The genes of an individual make up their genotype while their physical or mental characteristics (including reading) comprise the phenotype. Molecular geneticists have been interested in how individual differences in reading (and the 'dyslexia phenotype' in particular) relate to differences in the genotype between affected people with dyslexia and their unaffected relatives. Given that the genome comprises between 20,000 and 25,000 genes across 3 billion base pairs of DNA, this is no small challenge. And we should not forget that genes operate through the environment, environments vary between individuals, and genes interact with other genes as well.

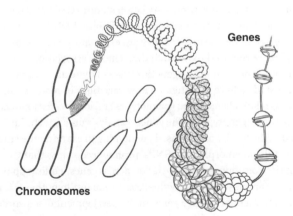

Genes

Chromosomes

15. **The genetic make-up of an individual is contained in the chromosomes. This diagram illustrates how chromosomes comprise strings of genes. Some of the candidate genes associated with dyslexia risk include ROBO1 and KIAA0139 on chromosome 6.**

The first approaches aimed at understanding the genetic basis of dyslexia were linkage studies. By closely comparing the DNA provided by individuals with dyslexia with that from biologically related individuals without dyslexia, it is possible to identify chromosome regions of increased similarity between affected individuals and hence plausible genetic differences which lead to differences in reading skills (a good reader vs a poor reader). This approach led to the identification of broad sections of chromosomes for dyslexia on chromosomes 1, 2, 3, 6, 15, and 18. Following up these studies using other techniques allows the identification of specific gene variants and 'candidate genes' in these regions, which appear to be involved in the development of dyslexia. However, the association between a candidate gene and aspects of the dyslexic profile is relatively weak in most cases. Furthermore, findings have not always been replicated and it seems likely that some of the original associations may hold only for subgroups of individuals.

Following on from linkage studies, attention turned to large-scale studies called genome-wide association studies (GWAS). These studies look for correlations between millions of DNA variations and behavioural measures; as they are exploratory, very large samples are required to avoid finding chance associations. In an attempt to understand the genetic causes of dyslexia, several GWAS studies have investigated how variations in reading and reading-related behaviours (phenotypes) relate to variations across the genome (genotypes). The genetic analysis uses a technique called high-density array-based genotyping to examine the single nucleotide polymorphisms (SNPs, pronounced snips) that comprise common genetic variation across genes. Follow-up in selected samples (even individual cases) can test hypotheses about the involvement of specific genes in the development of a disorder. At the present time, although associations have been discovered between some candidate genes and dyslexia, there have been few replications and there is still uncertainty surrounding the findings.

In short, we know that dyslexia is a heritable condition but we still have a long way to go before understanding its genetic basis. Future studies will make use of new and improved techniques for genetic analysis, but, as our three cases illustrate, the pattern of inheritance is not straightforward and there is much variability across individuals with dyslexia.

What is the role of the environment in the genesis of dyslexia?

If dyslexia is strongly related to genetic effects, why is the environment important? One of the biggest fallacies in popular understanding of genetics is that our genes determine our destiny. Genes act through the environment and the environment has a profound influence on our development. Body builders can change their shape through exercise; health and cognition can be affected by malnourishment; and, as studies of illiterate people show us, the brain can be shaped by literacy. A very clear demonstration comes from the inherited disorder of *phenylketonuria* (PKU). If not treated, PKU leads to a build-up of a substance called phenylalanine in the blood stream which then affects the metabolism of proteins and, in turn, causes damage to the brain. Fortunately, there is an infant blood screening test for PKU (known as the heel prick test) which allows early detection. At one time, babies with PKU grew up to develop learning disabilities; now, provided they are given a low-protein diet, they can develop normally.

Dyslexia is by no means as serious a condition as PKU, nor is there any evidence that it can be ameliorated by diet or medicine; however, the environment that children at risk of dyslexia experience can have a considerable effect on their literacy development and educational attainment. And later, the way it is managed can have an important effect not only on attainment but also on academic self-esteem and adult well-being. So we turn now to examine some of the factors which can potentially moderate the impact of dyslexia.

'It's the environment, stupid!'

Coining the phrase, 'It's the environment, stupid', the editor of a major journal argued that the missing link in our understanding of the genetic basis of many child psychiatric problems was the environment. So, what is the role of the environment in the development of dyslexia? It is well attested that environmental effects on child development are strong and learning to read is a particular example. Children who are brought up in home environments which are rich in literacy show faster reading development and schooling can have major effects on educational attainments. More generally, the culture in which we are born conditions the values that society place on literacy. How can we make sense of all of these effects?

In his classic work on the 'ecology' of development, Ulrich Bronfenbrenner proposed that the child is at the centre of a nested set of environmental influences—a Russian doll analogy. He used the terms microsystem, mesosystem, exosystem, and macrosystem to refer to these influences which he proposed were arranged hierarchically. He also argued that there are reciprocal interactions between them. In this view, the developing person is an active participant in their own development.

In applying this framework to dyslexia, we might consider the home literacy environment a 'microsystem' in which the child's individual interactions with parents and siblings, foster or constrain the development of language and set the stage for reading. We can then think of the school and within it the reading curriculum as a mesosystem, while home–school liaison reflects interactions between micro- and mesosystems. The exosystem refers to the effects of the community or neighbourhood in which a child is born. The exosystem typically reflects socio-economic circumstances and may contribute to the well-known social gradient in reading attainment. In terms of interactions, community resources are reduced in low-income neighbourhoods, with knock-on effects for the quality of schools and on the knowledge and cultural experience the child brings to the task of reading. Finally, the macrosystem will reflect the wider beliefs and values of the society and dictate educational policy. The language of learning is also part of the macrosystem. Figure 16 uses the framework to show some of the environmental factors that impinge on the developing reader.

Most research which is relevant to the impact of the environment on dyslexia focuses on the micro- and mesosystems. However, we should be mindful of the wider cultural context—the macrosystem. We have already considered how differences among writing systems influence the ease with which children learn to read.

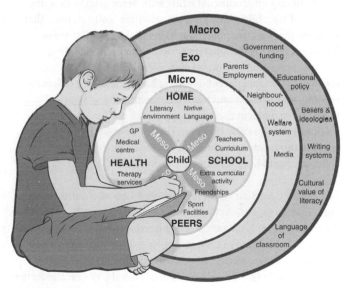

16. An illustration depicting influences on literacy within Bronfenbrenner's framework.

A child's difficulties in learning to read are likely to be magnified if they are raised in an environment which is multilingual or where the curriculum is delivered in a non-native language. Similarly, there will be additional challenges when there is diglossia, the situation where two varieties of the same language are spoken within one community yet only one is used in school. In a society which values literacy, there will be limitations on job opportunities for parents with low levels of literacy; hence family resources will be fewer. In turn, the choice of home neighbourhood will inevitably be restricted by family income and this will often dictate the quality of schools children attend. Sadly, a cycle of disadvantage may close off the kinds of interventions which best support the additional needs of a child with dyslexia.

Home literacy environment

Home literacy environment (HLE) is the term used to describe aspects of the child's background, activities, and interests that promote literacy development at home in the broadest sense. Measures of HLE include family demographics, including parental education and occupational levels; literary activities in the home including parental reading habits; teaching of letters, reading, and writing; and more passive influences, such as books in the home. Each of these is an important predictor of a child's reading-related skills. However, the active and interactive components, such as the amount of time spent reading with the child, appear to have the strongest influence.

In a classic Canadian study, researchers followed children from kindergarten (ages 5–6) through to Grade 3 (ages 8–9) to examine the impact of HLE on early reading development. Two aspects of the home literacy environment were measured in kindergarten: informal activities around storybook exposure, as assessed by parents' knowledge of children's book titles and authors, and formal activities involving the direct instruction of reading-related skills.

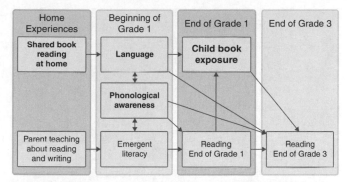

17. Senechal and LeFevere's model showing the influences of home literacy environment.

These two practices predicted different child skills (see Figure 17). Storybook exposure—talking with your child about books—was associated with individual differences in children's language comprehension. In contrast, direct instruction about print and letters was associated with emergent decoding and invented spelling. Interestingly, neither aspect of the home literacy environment directly predicted phonological awareness, yet both early literacy and language were associated with this important precursor of reading.

Consistent with many previous studies, individual differences in early literacy and phonological awareness in kindergarten went on to predict reading in Grade 1 and, in turn, individual differences in reading at this stage predicted reading in Grade 3. However, there were additional child predictors of reading outcome, namely Grade 1 language comprehension and the frequency with which the children were observed reading to themselves. The findings highlight two different environmental influences on reading skills in primary school: the home literacy environment provided by parents and the child's own choice of literary activities, sometimes called print exposure. Print exposure refers to the frequency of reading

18. Edouard Vuillard's *In the Library*: a perfect home learning environment?

outside the curriculum, usually referred to as 'reading for pleasure' (see Figure 18), and children with dyslexia tend to do this less.

The children who were followed in this study were from middle-class homes and it is fair to assume that, for the majority, the family was highly literate. It is reasonable to expect that the home literacy environment in a family in which one parent is dyslexic is going to be different from that of a family of avid readers. If reading is effortful, you are much less likely to enjoy a book, to read a newspaper, or to go to the library than to pursue activities which do not require reading, such as active sports or catching up with the news on TV.

Studies of the home literacy environment in dyslexia are sparse; however, after socio-economic circumstances are controlled, the environment in dyslexic families is not reported to differ greatly from the 'norm', although trends reflect less interest in reading. Counterintuitively perhaps (as it might be assumed they would not choose reading activities), there is also a suggestion that parents in 'dyslexic families' spend more time actively teaching their children, particularly about letters, than parents in control families. There is also some evidence that storybook reading is a protective activity for 'at-risk children'. In our Wellcome Language and Reading Project we showed that storybook reading can promote phonological awareness as well as reading. We also showed that the home literacy environment mediates the impact of socio-economic circumstances on readiness for learning in school. A more salutary finding is that the literacy and language skills a parent brings to the home (their own genes working through the environment) have a powerful influence on children's reading and language.

As well as assessing the children, we measured the language and literacy skills of each of the parents. In a model of the relationships between maternal skills, home literacy environment, and children's language and reading, we found firstly that maternal language predicted children's language and secondly that maternal phonological skills predicted children's word reading and spelling abilities. We also showed that maternal skills predicted informal but not formal aspects of the home literacy environment, that is, storybook exposure but not the tendency to teach about literacy in a more formal way. Importantly, after accounting for variations in maternal language, storybook exposure was no longer a significant predictor of children's reading or language whereas direct literacy instruction remained a predictor of children's reading/spelling skills. It seems, therefore, that the relationship between early informal home literacy activities and children's language and reading skills is largely accounted for by maternal skills, which may reflect genetic influences from mother to child rather than environmental influences.

Research on the home literacy environment in families with dyslexia is still in its early stages and more research is required to replicate the effects that have been reported. Future research needs also to go beyond ratings of the *quantity* of home literacy activities to include measures of the *quality* of home literacy interactions. There is also a need for research evaluating whether changing the practices of parents with dyslexia will enable their children to circumvent reading difficulties.

The effects of school

Schools are complex organizations and therefore it is difficult to assess their effects on individual children's reading skills. Research on school effectiveness aims to address the impact of schools on a range of educational outcomes, but there are numerous problems to be solved. How, for example, can we measure school 'quality', classroom organization, or teacher attitudes? Furthermore, how can we take account of the effects of the socio-political context or the effects of neighbouring schools on a school's attainments? Notwithstanding these problems, even when pupil characteristics at intake are taken into account, schools can make a difference to children's outcomes. However, such effects are on overall attainment—we don't yet know how well children with dyslexia thrive in different school settings. Anecdotal evidence suggests that specialist provision, including specialist dyslexia schools, can alter the outcomes for children with severe dyslexia, but good data are lacking; some of these effects may be on self-esteem and well-being rather than on educational attainments.

We need to try to learn more about the roles schools can play in improving the lot of children with dyslexia. Small steps are being made by national organizations which encourage diversity in teaching and learning. In a 'dyslexia-friendly' school, everyone from the headteacher to the caretaker and cooks is aware of the issues surrounding dyslexia. The quality of learning is ensured for the person with dyslexia and there is a close partnership between teachers and parents in supporting the needs of the dyslexic pupil. It is undoubtedly important for a school to aim for these standards but it is much more difficult to show a measurable impact on an individual child with dyslexia.

The effects of teaching and learning

At the micro-level, there is a large body of evidence showing that structured reading intervention can improve a child's reading skills. We will discuss 'what works' for dyslexia in Chapter 6; for the moment we simply note that it is an important environmental influence. We also note the importance of thinking about the effects of teaching and learning on dyslexia more broadly. Intervention programmes target specific skills—for most children with dyslexia, the focus is on developing reading and spelling skills, and rightly so. However, it is important also to ensure that the environment is adjusted to take account of both the consequences of dyslexia and the ongoing difficulties that affect functioning in the school and, later, the work environment. Many children with dyslexia also have problems learning arithmetic—Misha and both her sisters have mathematical difficulties; she is also a timid child and this sets her back further in the domain of numeracy where a particular anxiety around mathematics is a known phenomenon. Bobby is also having difficulty in learning his tables but he seems to have a good grasp of numbers. It is important to provide support to ensure his difficulties with basic calculation do not prevent him progressing further since already he is showing an interest in science and engineering where he will need to be mathematically adept.

It is many years since Harry was in full-time education. Although he received a lot of support with reading and writing from his parents and his tutor, his schools were less sympathetic and never really gave him much allowance for his difficulties. It is fair to say that being dyslexic knocked his confidence and he ended up with low academic self-concept: he could have gone on to further study but chose not to. Bobby is already getting turned off education, with conduct problems evident as a result of his frustration. There is absolutely no reason why dyslexia should have this wider impact on behaviour and emotional adjustment: with the advent of technology, schools should be able to provide appropriate contexts for learning for all children with special needs.

Genes select their environments

The study of the genetics of dyslexia is in some ways more advanced than the study of the environments that influence dyslexia. However, these two potentially different explanations for individual differences in reading are not entirely separable. Consideration of what is known as gene–environment correlation is particularly important for understanding dyslexia. Gene–environment correlation (r*GE*) refers to the influence of genes *working through* the environment. In the case of dyslexia, not only does each parent share on average 50 per cent of their genes with their child, but also they will bring to the task of child rearing an environment that is associated with their genotype (which might be a poor literacy environment). This is an example of passive r*GE*. A second type of gene–environment correlation is evocative, that is, it evokes particular interpersonal interactions. An example would be that of a child who has inherited a genetic risk for dyslexia who may wish to be read to less often than a child not at family risk. Finally, an active r*GE* correlation refers to the situation in which a child with dyslexia selects for themselves an environment in which there is little exposure to print (and may, for example, prefer active pursuits). Thus, a so-called 'environmental' factor such as how much a child reads may itself be heritable (indeed there is emerging evidence that this is so). No study has yet been able to disentangle genetic from r*GE* effects in dyslexia and there is a dearth of research investigating what are likely to be powerful effects of the child's genes in their engagement with, and their enjoyment of, interactions involving literacy.

Chapter 5
The dyslexic brain

All behaviour, including reading, is controlled by the brain. It is therefore natural to ask: are there differences in brain structure or function in dyslexia that cause difficulties in learning to read?

While initial pioneering work had suggested that dyslexia, or congenital word blindness, had a neurological origin, the first direct evidence of brain differences in dyslexia was reported by researchers working in Boston, USA. In a series of studies of post-mortem brain samples of five males with a history of dyslexia, this team found malformations, called ectopias, in layers of the brain's cortex located primarily in frontal and left language regions. They suggested that these microscopic malformations were the result of the faulty migration of nerve cells (neurons) during pre-natal development. In addition, they reported atypical symmetry in the region of the *planum temporale*.

These original findings have been disputed, not least because little is known about the *actual* skills of the dyslexic people whose brains were analysed. Furthermore, animal research investigating the role of dyslexia candidate genes in brain development has also failed to support the initial hypothesis about the migration of nerve cells. An interesting blog on the topic (BishopBlog) contains more information.

Neuroimaging as a tool for investigating the brain

It is now some forty years since this classic work on the dyslexic brain. In this time, techniques for examining the living brain have been developed and are still developing. It is now possible to image the structure and function of the brain in great detail and this has allowed progress to be made in understanding the brain regions that are engaged during reading. The main brain imaging techniques in current use include: *magnetic resonance imaging* (MRI) to examine the brain's structure (the distribution of grey (nerve cell bodies) and white (nerve fibres) matter); *diffusion tensor imaging* (DTI) to investigate the brain's wiring (tracts of nerve fibres which transmit activation between nerve cells); *functional magnetic resonance imaging* (fMRI) to assess patterns of brain activation during processing, which are inferred from changes in cerebral blood flow reflecting increased metabolic activity in 'active' nerve cells; and *magnetoencephalography* (MEG) and *electroencephalography* (EEG) used to measure the timing of electrical activity in the brain. We will focus for the moment on measures of brain function, noting that differences in brain structure between dyslexic and non-impaired readers have been confirmed in left language regions, as was hypothesized following the early studies using post-mortem samples.

The mechanism underlying functional brain imaging can be conceptualized quite simply. When a cognitive task requires processing by a given brain system, the blood flow to that brain system increases, bringing with it the oxygen needed for the task (analogous to the increase in blood flow to the muscles experienced during physical exercise). Changes in blood flow and oxygen levels in the blood can then be used to investigate the regions of the brain that are active during a task such as reading. Technologies such as MEG and EEG also reveal the timing (in milliseconds) of the processes which are engaged in the task.

The earliest studies to use functional brain imaging to investigate dyslexia used a technique called PET (positron emission tomography) and these studies only involved adults. Together they confirmed differences between dyslexic and normal readers in left hemisphere regions involved in language processing, and one, by Paulesu and colleagues, proposed some kind of 'disconnection' between regions involved in phonological processing and word recognition. There were, however, inevitably limitations to these pioneering studies and they were experimental in the sense that they compared dyslexic and normal reader groups in the absence of much information about the normally functioning reading brain or how it develops. A programme of research in Connecticut by Bennett and Sally Shaywitz, Ken Pugh, and their colleagues (and others) has told us a great deal about the brain basis of reading in the 'typical' case, against which we now can interpret the brain differences observed in dyslexia.

The brain's network for reading

Reading involves translating visual letter sequences into sounds and meaning. Three main systems are involved (see Figure 19). The first is a system towards the back of the brain; here parts of the temporal and parietal cortex appear crucial for assembling the phonological codes of words. The second is a system called the 'word form area', which is thought to contain an important area for word recognition (as opposed to decoding); this is also in the temporal region but overlapping with the visual cortex. A third region toward the front of the brain is also activated; this area (the inferior frontal gyrus) is responsible for speech production and is active not only during reading aloud but also during silent reading. Figure 19 reminds us that the brain basis of reading is 'parasitic' on brain structures which evolved for different reasons—namely in the service of speech production, language comprehension, and vision—a process which has been referred to as 'neuronal recycling'.

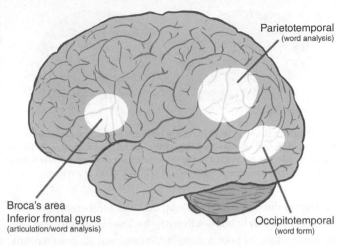

Parietotemporal
(word analysis)

Broca's area
Inferior frontal gyrus
(articulation/word analysis)

Occipitotemporal
(word form)

19. The main brain regions involved in reading; from Shaywitz & Shaywitz (2008).

The dyslexic brain

Turning now to imaging studies of dyslexia, we find considerable consensus that the two 'hot spots' for reading towards the back of the brain show lower activation in poor readers compared with normal readers (see Figure 20).

Furthermore, disruption of this network appears to be associated with a shift in activation to other brain regions, including the area at the front of the brain. Regions in the right hemisphere are also active in dyslexia as compared to typical reading which primarily engages left hemisphere systems. Such increased activity in the right hemisphere may reflect compensatory processes brought to bear by the dyslexic reader in the face of decoding difficulty.

The *Connecticut Longitudinal Study* investigated patterns of brain activation in two groups of people aged 18–22 who, as children, had been identified as dyslexic. One group—the persistently poor readers—had continued to experience reading

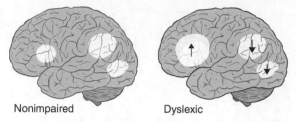

Nonimpaired   Dyslexic

20. Diagram showing levels of brain activation (paler areas) during reading in typical readers (left of picture) and dyslexic readers (right of picture). The frontal region in the dyslexic brain shows relatively more activation, the posterior regions show relatively less activation.

difficulties through school while others—the compensated readers (who were accurate but not fluent)—had no longer satisfied research criteria for poor reading by Grades 9 and 10. In a nonword reading task, both groups showed under-activation in neural regions for reading in the left posterior regions of the brain when compared with non-impaired readers from the same study. However, the compensated readers also activated right frontal regions more than both of the other groups. What this suggests is that they were engaging compensatory neural systems in order to read the nonwords.

The performance of the two 'poor reader' groups also diverged in a reading task involving words. Perhaps counterintuitively, the persistently poor readers showed similar levels of activation to typical readers in posterior brain regions; however, further investigation revealed that there were differences in the ways in which this region was connected with other regions. It seemed that the persistently poor readers were engaging a memory network to read words holistically, whereas proficient readers were using analytic word identification strategies.

Examining behavioural and demographic data from the two groups of poor readers at the start of the study provides food for thought: the compensated poor readers were of higher IQ than the persistently poor readers and they also attended more advantaged schools. It could be that the group who had reached normal levels of reading accuracy had fewer co-occurring difficulties—and hence did better on IQ tests—or it could be that they had been taught better. The brain data suggest the two groups of children have followed different developmental pathways; what remains unclear is the extent to which their trajectories were determined by pre-existing differences in brain structure or whether the differences in brain processes reflect differences in the extent to which the two groups had mastered reading.

Is the brain's signature for dyslexia the same across languages?

To the extent that the task of reading differs between languages, one might expect that the brain regions involved would also differ. Learning to read in English takes longer than learning to read in other alphabetic languages because it contains many irregular forms, such as 'school', 'sign', 'broad'. In contrast, languages such as German or Spanish are more regular and the majority of letter-sound rules or mappings they contain are consistent, at least for reading (see Chapter 2). A classic study suggested that, despite these differences, there was 'biological unity' of dyslexia across languages. In a study comparing university students with dyslexia who were readers of English, French, or Italian, there were no between-language differences in brain activation during reading although the three language groups did differ in their reading speed; this was faster for the Italian dyslexics than for the French and the English group.

The people with dyslexia studied in the cross-language study of dyslexia exhibited the now well-replicated under-activation of large areas of left temporal and occipital brain regions at the back of the brain but with no evidence of regions of over-activation. Subsequent studies following this work have found support for this notion of 'biological unity' but have also noted some language-specific aspects to the so-called 'neural signature' of dyslexia. A meta-analysis of imaging data from fourteen studies in English and fourteen studies in regular orthographies (including Dutch, German, Italian, and Swedish) confirms that reduced activation of left brain regions, including the word form area, is a universal feature of dyslexia. However, there are differences between English and the regular orthographies in the spatial extent and location of clusters of over- and under-activation. Arguably this is to be expected given cross-linguistic differences between writing systems and the demands they place on decoding.

What about a very different writing system like Chinese? Chinese characters are complex visuo-spatial forms which map to syllables and have a closer relationship to meaning (morphemes) than do the graphic units of the alphabetic writing systems. A brain imaging study directly comparing patterns of brain activity for monolingual English and Chinese readers aged 13–16 years while they performed a semantic matching task involving printed words (or pictures) revealed interesting findings: during reading, Chinese normal readers activated frontal regions more than English readers, whereas English readers activated posterior temporal regions more. The most likely explanation of this lies in the fact that in Chinese there is a direct mapping from symbol to word pronunciation whereas in English phonological codes are activated. More puzzling is that the dyslexic readers showed neither the Chinese-specific nor the English-specific differences in the frontal and posterior regions. The authors conclude that orthography-specific reading strategies that are culturally determined are less apparent when reading is less efficient. Put another way, learning to read refines brain networks in order to adapt them for the language of learning and this does not happen to the same extent in dyslexia irrespective of the language.

Does literacy change the brain?

The comparison of 'dyslexic' and 'non-dyslexic' brains is driven by the quest to find a biological cause of dyslexic learning difficulties. However, as the cross-linguistic findings reveal, there is a problem—and that is that literacy changes the brain. We have thus far focused on functional changes in brain activation that correlate with reading skill. However, since brain activity is simply a reflection of differences in cognitive processes, we now turn to consider the impact of learning to read on aspects of brain structure.

All aspects of learning lead to changes in brain structure. By brain structure we mean the density of nerve cells and the number and length of the connections between them (the wiring). During normal development, changes in brain structure consequent to literacy cannot easily be separated from developmental changes that are attributable to other maturational or social processes. In rare cases, however, studying adults who learn to read late in life offers an opportunity to examine brain changes following the onset of literacy when in all other respects maturation is complete.

Just such an opportunity occurred in Colombia where illiterate adults who had received no formal education returned to society after a protracted period of warfare and were offered the chance of learning to read. This was an opportunity to compare adults who achieved literacy in their 20s (late-literates) with those who remained illiterate, and with a comparison group from the same Spanish-speaking population who had learned to read as children. The research team used a technique called voxel-based morphometry to compare differences in brain structure between those groups.

First, examining the language regions towards the back of the brain that form the reading network, the researchers found increased grey matter in the late-literates compared with illiterates of the same age. Second, they found increased white matter indicating a stronger connection in areas of the *corpus callosum* that allows communication between the two sides of the brain. Similar changes have previously been observed in the brains of children as they learn to read. Although further research is needed to understand the role of this evident coupling between left and right brain structures, what seems clear is that it is a *consequence* of literacy and not a *prerequisite* for it to develop.

Brain imaging as a predictor?

Can brain imaging help us to predict individual differences in reading development? Although the problem of disentangling causes from consequences is now well recognized by researchers who use brain imaging methods, there remains the intriguing question of whether brain differences might make it easier for some children to learn to read than others. One way of addressing this question is to compare children with dyslexia with younger peers who are reading at the same level; through this method reading experience is equated so any brain differences that are found can be attributed to dyslexia. A second approach is to conduct longitudinal studies which investigate the significance of brain measures as predictors of individual differences in reading skill. These strategies are at the core of the research programme led by Fumiko Hoeft in the US.

Using the first approach, brain processing in children with dyslexia was compared with that of two groups of typical readers. One of these was of same age (age-controls) and the other of children reading at the same level as the children with dyslexia (reading ability-controls). Each child was required to make rhyme judgements about printed words by pressing a button while in the scanner (e.g. *boat–coat* = RHYME; *warm–harm* = DON'T RHYME). During this task, the children with dyslexia showed reduced activation compared with both groups of controls in left posterior brain regions and in five other brain regions. A further finding was that the activity in the posterior brain regions correlated with performance on standardized reading tests. This confirmed the hypothesis that developmental changes in brain activation in these key areas are associated with increases in reading ability. However, since the children with dyslexia showed even less activation here than their younger peers (RA-controls), we can infer that the lower levels of brain activity are not just a correlate of a low level of reading. Rather, this reduced activation suggests that children with dyslexia are on a 'different' trajectory of development as they learn to read.

The next step was to compare the brain structure of dyslexic readers with that of age- and RA-controls in the regions identified as under-active in dyslexia in fMRI. A region of interest was the area of frontal cortex which is thought to be over-active in dyslexia. This is important because differences in brain structure can lead to differences in brain-activation patterns. The results were strikingly complementary to those from functional imaging: for the children with dyslexia, there was reduced grey matter volume in the language areas which typically show

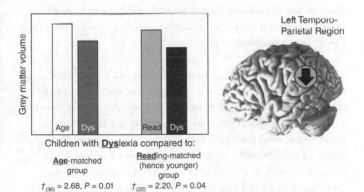

Left Temporo-Parietal Region

Grey matter volume

Age | Dys | Read | Dys

Children with **Dys**lexia compared to:

Age-matched group
$t_{(36)} = 2.68$, $P = 0.01$

Reading-matched (hence younger) group
$t_{(22)} = 2.20$, $P = 0.04$

21. **Bar graph showing significantly reduced grey matter volume in the dyslexic group relative to the age-matched and reading-matched groups.**

under-activation—and this was relative to both age- and RA-controls (see Figure 21). However, differences in the grey matter in the frontal regions which typically show over-activation were only significant relative to age and not to RA-controls. This latter finding implies that over-activity is a function of reading level rather than of dyslexia per se. Thus, increased activity in frontal regions may be best conceptualized as being associated with a process which serves to facilitate reading when decoding is effortful. These findings represent a significant step in identifying a plausible biological cause of dyslexic learning difficulties in left brain regions involved in phonological storage and in mapping between orthography and phonology.

The research team went on to investigate the role of left- and right-brain systems in predicting reading outcomes using a more robust longitudinal approach. This involved following children with and without dyslexia for two and a half years, taking both behavioural and brain measures with the aim of predicting reading development. At the start of the study, children were scanned while completing a written rhyme-judgement task like the one just described. Brain images were analysed to identify both brain activation and brain structure in regions of interest. None of the behavioural measures predicted growth in reading. However, measures of brain structure and function did—and for the dyslexic group only.

The measures of interest were of activation in left and right frontal regions and of structure in a tract of nerve fibres called the *arcuate fasciculus*, again in both hemispheres. This structure is a kind of 'temporal pathway' connecting the frontal and parieto-temporal 'hot spots' (see Figure 22A). A novel finding was that children with dyslexia who improved the most in reading showed more activation in the right frontal cortex (see Figure 22B) and greater white matter integrity in the right arcuate fasciculus (see Figure 22C) at baseline.

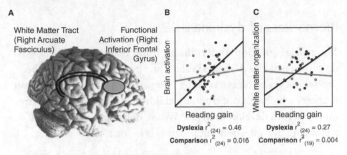

A White Matter Tract (Right Arcuate Fasciculus) Functional Activation (Right Inferior Frontal Gyrus)

B Brain activation / Reading gain

Dyslexia $r^2_{(24)}$ = 0.46
Comparison $r^2_{(24)}$ = 0.016

C White matter organization / Reading gain

Dyslexia $r^2_{(24)}$ = 0.27
Comparison $r^2_{(19)}$ = 0.004

22. **(A) Brain regions implicated in reading gains in dyslexia in right inferior frontal gyrus, and white matter organization in right arcuate fasciculus. Graphs showing (B) an association between reading gains and brain activation in right inferior frontal gyrus and (C) an association between reading gains and white matter organization in right arcuate fasciculus (dyslexia group (black), comparison group (grey)).**

To investigate this issue further, the research team focused on the development of brain structure in 5–6-year-old children. In particular, they examined the structure of the 'temporal pathway' (called the arcuate fasciculus). The children also completed assessments of pre-reading and cognitive skills in kindergarten and were reassessed in Grade 3 on reading measures. Together, measures of pre-literacy and a dynamic measure of the development in brain structure over time accounted for 56 per cent of the variability in reading outcome at Grade 3. Moreover, it was change in white matter density in the pathway which mattered most. In short, this study showed that the growth of the pathway—the connections linking frontal and temporo-parietal brain areas—predicts individual differences in reading, after controlling for pre-reading skills in kindergarten and other demographic measures such as socio-economic status, home literacy environment, and family history of reading problems. The authors suggest that growth of the fibres in the temporal pathway might be regarded as a marker of brain plasticity in the region required for phonological processing and word learning. It is plausible that such plasticity is under genetic influence.

Biomarkers of dyslexia risk?

The crucial question underpinning brain research in dyslexia is: do children at risk of dyslexia show any brain differences in the pre-school years, before reading instruction? Could there be brain markers which can differentiate children at family risk who are more likely to develop dyslexia? We are definitely some way off answering this question but progress is being made.

Recent years have seen a growing use of EEG to investigate cognitive processing very early in development. This approach is rather different from the one we have been discussing but is particularly suitable for assessing infants and toddlers and can even be used to test brain processing in sleeping babies! Electrodes placed on the child's head record the timing of brain responses to different types of stimuli and data are summed over many trials to assess the child's sensitivity to features of the stimuli. These so-called event-related potentials (ERPs) provide sensitive measures of the timing of different stages of cognitive processing, such as those required for reading.

In pioneering studies, ERPs were recorded from the brains of newborn infants produced in response to random sequences of speech and non-speech sounds. Data were then used to predict the reading outcomes of these infants some eight years later when they were classified into three groups: 24 normal readers, 17 dyslexic readers, and 7 poor readers (with lower IQ). The data discriminated between the groups with 81.25 per cent accuracy and with 76.5 per cent of the dyslexic readers correctly classified.

Similar methods have been used in two longitudinal studies of children at family risk of dyslexia, the Jyvvaskla study in Finland and the Dutch Family Study in the Netherlands. The studies have yielded some interesting findings. In addition to observing differences between 'at-risk' and not 'at-risk' infants and preschoolers in aspects of auditory and speech perception, some of these studies report weak correlations between these measures and later measures of phonological skills, reading, and spelling. However, study samples are small and we have little evidence as yet that such responses in the newborn period can predict which children will become dyslexic.

Later in a child's development, at the stage when children are just beginning to learn to read, research points to relationships between reading and aspects of brain structure in critical language areas, and to differences between children at family risk of dyslexia and controls. Two findings stand out. First, cortical thickness in left brain reading-related areas is lower among children at family risk, whereas the surface area of right cortical regions implicated in dyslexia is higher. Second, maternal rather than paternal history of dyslexia is a predictor of reduced grey matter in language-related regions of the left hemisphere but not of white matter density. The more severe the mother's history of reading problems, the more reduced the cortical surface. Further research is certainly needed to pin this finding down, but findings from studies of children at family risk of dyslexia offer intriguing hypotheses about how brain structure might reflect the influence of genes on learning to read and the likelihood of dyslexia.

Chapter 6
What works for dyslexia?

What every parent wants to know and what every adult with dyslexia asks is: 'What can we do about dyslexia?' The internet is replete with 'cures', which do a great disservice to people with dyslexia and their families: there is no 'quick fix' or cure for dyslexia; dyslexia is a lifelong condition. Nevertheless, there are ways of helping to improve reading and spelling as well as ways to get around some of the problems that come with dyslexia. In addition, early intervention can set a child on to the right track to developing adequate literacy skills.

In order to provide advice on what works we need evidence-based approaches. By 'evidence-based' interventions we mean those that have been shown to be effective in robust evaluations. By and large, these are programmes that have been designed with reference to a causal theory—in essence, if we know 'what' is causing the problem, this tells us 'what' needs improving. Interventions for dyslexia should aim to improve the deficient process or processes that have led to the reading problem. Unfortunately, not all dyslexia interventions have an evidence base.

Is diagnosis of dyslexia the starting point?

Although governments are prone to mandate particular approaches, it is generally agreed that phonics instruction provides the best way into successful decoding for all children but that there also needs to be a balanced approach to literacy teaching in the mainstream classroom. A nice example of a framework for thinking about the various component skills which a child needs to become a fluent reader is shown in Figure 23.

The first step to intervention for any kind of problem is identification of a child's difficulties. Particularly for a child at risk of dyslexia, it is important to monitor progress through the early stages of reading instruction and to intervene as soon as possible; what is not necessary is a formal diagnosis of dyslexia. The tendency to delay intervention until a specialist confirms the child is 'dyslexic' has thwarted progress: it makes perfect sense to help a child who is struggling as soon as possible. In this way we can avoid a downward spiral of frustration and distress.

Screening tests for dyslexia have become popular in schools. Good schools want to do all they can to identify children at risk of dyslexia. However, it would be wrong to think that screening using formal tests is the only way forward—one-off assessments or screens can over-identify children with difficulties; this is a waste of resources. Our Wellcome Language and Reading Project showed that in preschool, the best predictor of whether or not a child will develop dyslexia is 'family risk': if there is already dyslexia in the family, the probability of a child becoming dyslexic is increased and the prediction is better than from formal measures at early ages. The situation changes after school entry. By age 5, dyslexia can be predicted well by a child's letter knowledge, phoneme awareness, and performance on the rapid naming test (the so-called triple foundation). Even then, family risk adds further to the probability of a child developing persistent difficulties.

Dyslexia is a specific difficulty in learning to decode and to spell. So dyslexia can be suspected when a child shows poor reading and spelling. In only the rare case will a teacher *not* know who in their

23. A balanced approach to early literacy development.

class is not progressing at the expected rate for their age. In my view, teachers need to be empowered to pick out children at risk of dyslexia by using their own skilled observations of a child's reading and writing.

Screening in the mainstream classroom

A few years ago, the UK government introduced a policy of teaching systematic phonics to all children at school entry. Shortly afterwards, in 2012, they introduced a Phonics Screening Check at the end of Year 1 for all children (after two years of formal reading instruction). The check comprises twenty words and twenty nonwords for reading aloud and a proficiency level is set regarding the expected level to be achieved. As it happened, at the time of the nationwide introduction of the check, all of the Year 1 teachers in the York area had been trained by the Literacy Consultant to make careful observations of the progress of their pupils through the stages of phonics teaching and to record these formally. So for every child, in every school, it was possible to compare teachers' ratings of phonics progress in addition to performance on the government's phonics screening check. This offered the perfect opportunity to validate the screening check against teacher judgements.

Our findings were salutary. Children's scores on the government phonics screening check correlated strongly with their performance on the standardized reading tests we administered, confirming the validity of the measure. Most interestingly, scores on the phonics screening check were predicted just as well by teachers' observations as by standardized tests, confirming that the teachers in our study had been well trained and properly supported to use observations to rate their pupils' progress. The scale the teachers used was part of the 'Letters and Sounds' reading curriculum recommended by the Rose Review of the teaching of reading (see Box 1). The results showed that, if they are properly supported, teachers can feel confident about identifying children in their class who are slow to acquire phonic skills and hence are at risk of dyslexia.

Tiers of intervention

The Rose Review of dyslexia suggested a three-tier system of intervention for dyslexia (see Figure 24). Tier 1 represents

Box 1. Rating scale used by teachers to monitor children's progress through the UK Letters and Sounds Curriculum

Letters and Sounds Check

1. distinguish between different sounds in environment and phonemes; show awareness of rhyme and alliteration; blend and segment orally

2i. know about 6 grapheme–phoneme correspondences (GPCs). Blend and segment words with simple sound structures (vowel–consonant (VC) and consonant–vowel–consonant (CVC)) and captions with letters

2ii. know ~19 GPCs. Blend/segment as before; know some tricky words

3. know one way of representing each of 42 phonemes. Blend and segment CVC words including graphemes of more than one letter, two-syllable words, and captions. Read and spell tricky words

4. blend adjacent consonants in words and apply when reading unfamiliar texts. Segment adjacent consonants and apply to spelling

5. know alternative ways of spelling/pronouncing graphemes. Blend/segment. Spell complex words using phonically plausible attempts

6. apply phonic skills and knowledge with increasing fluency when reading unfamiliar words in texts. Recognize and spell increasing number of complex words including applying rules for adding prefixes and suffixes.

Source: Department for Education, *Guidance Letters and sounds*, 2007. Contains public sector information licensed under the Open Government Licence v3.0.

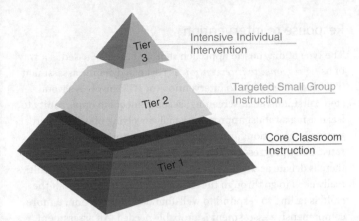

24. Tiers of support within the 'response to intervention' approach.

well-structured phonics teaching in a language-rich curriculum in the mainstream classroom. For some children who come to school less well prepared for literacy than others, this may be sufficient to get them off to a good start. Tier 2 is for those children who have difficulties and are falling behind. It is typically provided to children in small groups and involves extra literacy support along similar lines to the mainstream curriculum but it is more intensive, plugging gaps and reinforcing new skills for about six weeks. Children who are still showing slow progress at this stage should now have a fuller assessment to try to work out why they are failing to progress and move on to Tier 3.

Our case, Bobby, is one such child who by this stage needed special input. He had already had 'catch-up' support to no avail and the urgency of intervention was underlined by his deteriorating patterns of behaviour. Since he had a history of slow talking and earlier speech problems, it was wise to assess his language skills more broadly to determine whether, like some 40 per cent of children with dyslexia, he also had a developmental disorder affecting spoken language.

Response to intervention

The type of diagnostic approach that we have discussed is a way of using *response to intervention* as part of a dynamic assessment of dyslexia. Response to intervention (or RTI) involves several steps: first, universal screening; second, adequate opportunity to learn using a robust approach (usually involving phonics); third, tiers of intervention; and last, ongoing monitoring to ensure satisfactory progress (which here means 'catching up'). However, there is debate as to whether children with more severe difficulties really need to go through the different stages. Regardless, if the child is failing to respond to well-founded intervention, a more comprehensive assessment is probably needed. An assessment should include well-standardized measures of word reading, word spelling, letter knowledge, and phoneme awareness (see Box 2). This provides a baseline from which to monitor further progress.

> **Box 2. Guidelines for a dyslexia assessment**
>
> **Guidelines for an Assessment of Dyslexia**
>
> A comprehensive assessment should be undertaken prior to Tier 3 intervention.
>
> Selected tests from sets A, B, and C should be included.
>
> Tests from D and E are optional.
>
> At earlier stages of assessment and monitoring, one test from A (reading) and one from B (spelling) could be given at 6-monthly intervals to evaluate response to intervention (some RTI approaches recommend particular tests).
>
> A. Reading Ability should be assessed comprehensively:
> - Letter knowledge (if required, names and sounds)
> - Single word reading—to assess reading accuracy

- Nonword reading—to assess decoding skill
- Timed word and nonword reading—to assess reading rate
- Reading comprehension—to assess prose reading accuracy and fluency, and understanding of text

B. Spelling and Writing should form part of the assessment:
- Single word spelling—to assess accuracy
- Free writing sample—to provide an assessment of spelling accuracy when writing, use of grammar, punctuation, and writing fluency
- Handwriting sample—to assess writing rate and letter formation

C. Phonological Skills:
- Phonological awareness—to assess the ability to segment and/or manipulate the phonemic structure of words
- Rapid naming—to assess verbal processing speed
- Nonword repetition or verbal short-term memory—to assess phonological memory skills

D. General Cognitive Ability:

Although IQ is not used in the definition of dyslexia, a test of general cognitive ability can provide clues as to the nature of the child or adult's difficulty.

- Poor vocabulary may suggest a need for further assessment of language skills
- Poor visuo-spatial difficulty may suggest a need for further assessment of motor skills

E. Number Skills:

Screening of arithmetic skills is also recommended for children with dyslexia given the frequent comorbidity of problems with mathematics.

Approaches to dyslexia remediation

For many years, educational practice in the field of dyslexia rested on the assumption that children with dyslexia needed a different approach from other poor readers. Inspired by the Orton–Gillingham–Stillman approach (see Figure 25), several structured programmes of remediation were developed in the UK and elsewhere, such as Alpha to Omega by Hornsby and Shear, the Hickey Approach, and the Bangor Dyslexia Teaching System. Many cohorts of specialist dyslexia teachers were trained to deliver these methods, usually on a one-to-one or one-to-two basis, and many children (and adults) have benefited from this form of teaching. The theoretical foundation of these approaches is sound—they are designed to be highly structured, systematic, and multisensory in order to get around dyslexic difficulties in memory and learning. I have used them myself under the tutelage of Beve Hornsby, one of the UK's pioneers of dyslexia. I would

25. The author teaching a child with dyslexia using the Orton–Gillingham–Stillman approach at Barts' Clinic in 1979.

certainly not wish to decry them. But in the absence of robust evidence we do not know why these approaches work (if they do). For instance, is it the structure or the multisensory aspects of the programme that helps learning, or is it the skill of the tutors who deliver the teaching (for sure, they are delivered by talented teachers)? Indeed, having help from someone who understands the condition and can adapt their teaching to the needs of the learner can itself provide an enormous boost to progress.

To answer the question 'what works?' it is necessary to run a study in which one group receives the intervention and another receives their usual diet of teaching.

Randomized controlled trials

The gold standard for evidence of efficacy of an intervention is the randomized controlled trial (RCT). Ideally, the interventions used to ameliorate dyslexia should have been evaluated in such a trial. Such trials are termed 'randomized' because children will be allocated 'at random' either to receive the intervention or to receive 'business as usual'; 'controlled' because the effects of the intervention for the group who receive it are compared with those for the 'business as usual' group who do not. RCTs are common in medicine but have been used much less often in education. Arguably, they are the only fair way of judging whether or not a new programme works and that is in the interests of all children.

The best evidence we have is that the most effective approaches to the remediation of dyslexia are those which contain integrated activities which target phoneme awareness, letter knowledge, and linkage of the two, and which also include practice to reinforce emergent decoding abilities and increase reading fluency. There is no magic bullet; the components of these interventions are the same components that comprise effective reading instruction for typical readers. However, they are more intense, often more individualized (although there is little evidence that one-to-one teaching is better than small-group) and usually delivered by skilled practitioners with experience of learning disabilities. For these interventions to work, practice is a crucial factor—practice, practice, and more practice!

My colleagues Peter Hatcher, Charles Hulme, and Andy Ellis conducted a pioneering study in which they compared three forms of intervention with 'business as usual' for 7-year-old children who were significantly behind their peers in reading. The interventions comprised structured reading intervention, phonological awareness training, or an integrated approach which trained phonological awareness in the context of reading from books. It was the latter approach, dubbed 'Sound Linkage', that was the most effective for reading after six months of intervention and at follow-up some nine months later.

The Sound Linkage approach is not unique and its features are replicated in many of the approaches used with children with dyslexia. We sometimes refer to it as a 'reading sandwich'. The lesson starts with reading and ends with reading (the slices of bread) and there is training in phoneme awareness, letter knowledge, and phonic linkage in the middle (the filling). The reading sections of the lesson are derived from Marie Clay's 'Reading Recovery' approach and use books that are graded for difficulty. A critical feature of the method is that the tutor delivering the lesson is trained to select books at the right level to support the child in practising and perfecting their emerging decoding skills. In each lesson, two books are used—an easy book for reading practice and a book at the 'instructional level'. The easy book is one the child has read before—usually in the last lesson—and can now read accurately; they reread it to increase sight vocabulary and hence reading fluency—this is important because reading practice should be enjoyable.

Selecting the instructional level book requires more preparation: the teacher chooses, from a graded set, a book which they think will challenge the child (but not so much that they want to give up). Vygotsky coined the phrase the 'zone of proximal development' to refer to skills that the child is almost ready to acquire, and this is what we mean here. To home in on the appropriate level of instructional text, the teacher selects a short passage from the book—up to about 100 words—and asks the child to read it, while they take a verbatim record of their reading—the 'running record'. Later the teacher analyses the record to calculate the reading accuracy of the child. The aim is to find a book the child can read with relatively few errors, conventionally about 94 per cent accuracy—this will be within their proximal zone. The tutor also uses the running record to consider what the obstacles to accuracy currently are and to identify specific teaching points. The book is used in the next lesson as reading material and the teacher gives the child support while they read, focusing on only one or two teaching points. Indeed, rather than bombarding the child with corrective feedback, positive reinforcement of good reading strategies will be provided. Once the instructional book is mastered, it becomes one of the 'easy' books for future sessions. The approach relies upon having a set of graded books in the classroom or dyslexia centre. Unfortunately, books tend to go out of print and it is important always for teachers to keep their eyes open for new titles and, if necessary, find help with setting their level.

The Sound Linkage approach also includes some work on writing. Depending on the stage the child has reached, this might simply involve writing a word to complete a sentence which the teacher has written to target a teaching point, or composing a couple of complete sentences. The purpose is to provide reinforcement of phoneme–grapheme linkages or, for the more advanced child, simple spelling rules. The Sound Linkage approach (referred to more recently as Reading Intervention, <http://www.cumbria.gov. uk/childrensservices/schoolsandlearning/reading/default.asp>) is particularly effective for poor readers who are still in the early stages of reading, sometimes doubling the rate of progress.

However, as an approach to spelling, it is less effective. Gains in spelling tend to be short term and more specific attention needs to be directed to emergent writing skills if gains are to be maintained.

Teaching spelling

Very few controlled trials have assessed the efficacy of approaches to the teaching of spelling and most of the data we have come from looking at the impact of reading interventions on spelling performance. However, spelling is not just a consequence of reading—spelling problems are usually much more persistent than reading difficulties and require specific interventions. Best practice in the field of dyslexia suggests that orthographic patterns need to be taught explicitly. Whereas a good reader may abstract the correspondences of sounds in the word with letters and letter strings implicitly, this does not happen spontaneously in dyslexia. Many years ago, Uta Frith pointed out that reading relies on partial cues (you don't need to take in all the letters to read correctly) but spelling relies on full cues. If a child relies on context to compensate for inefficient decoding (as many children with dyslexia do), attention to the letter-by-letter structures of words may be minimal. To spell, they will have to rely on transcribing the sounds in the words. This won't be easy if the child has problems segmenting words into phonemes or is not familiar with conventional and context-dependent spelling patterns.

Teaching spelling to individuals with dyslexia usually involves teaching them specific spelling patterns and reinforcing knowledge of these patterns through writing words either singly or in sentences and preferably both. Such teaching is highly structured, allowing for over-learning and considerable reinforcement by using the spellings in different contexts. Similarly, many children with dyslexia are helped by being taught morphological rules and conventions—how to write a verb in the past tense (add -*ed*), how to handle prefixes (*in*-; *un*-) and suffixes (*-ful*; *-tion*), and how to recognize similarities in meaning between words which are usually captured by the same spelling patterns (*heal-health*). Children with dyslexia can sometimes surprise their parents by their wealth of knowledge of etymology (the study of words' origins)—and they enjoy being taught these writing tricks. But as ever, practice is vital. There is no quick fix for poor spelling.

'Treatment resistors'

An issue for all effective interventions is what to do with children who don't respond, sometimes called 'treatment resistors'. We still have very little knowledge about how best to serve the needs of these children—primarily, the strategy appears to be more intensive intervention, though this is costly and the benefits are not known. In one study, we showed that some of the children who responded poorly to reading intervention did better after a period of further instruction along the same lines, supplemented by work on vocabulary. Our hunch is that these children had been failing to thrive because of undiagnosed language difficulties. Similarly, recent research suggests that interventions for attention deficit hyperactivity disorder (ADHD), including medication, can have a positive effect on the reading of children who are both dyslexic and inattentive. But the mechanisms are unknown and hence such interventions cannot yet be recommended with confidence. More generally, and especially for older children with dyslexia, there is an absence of evidence about what works. We still know too little about how best to increase reading fluency or to improve spelling and writing skills.

What doesn't work for dyslexia?

Sometimes, when progress is slow, or even stagnates, parents will turn to unproven treatments which provide hope (see Figure 26). Parents cannot be expected to be able to draw upon the skills needed to evaluate evidence that is posted on webpages. Sadly, they may

'Can't I just go back to the coloured overlay!?'

26. Hypothetical unproven intervention for dyslexia.

be misled into purchasing complementary therapies or 'cures' often dressed up in what has been termed 'neurobabble'. There really should be a *What Doesn't Work Clearing House*, not just a *What Works* one!

Two warnings

There is not space here to go into the myriad remedies that are said to help dyslexia. Instead we will discuss some approaches which have gained in popularity in recent years but which do not get to the heart of dyslexia.

First, as we have seen, dyslexia frequently co-occurs with other developmental disorders. It could be that these co-occurring (sometimes called comorbid) conditions add an additional obstacle to the educational progress of a child with dyslexia; it follows that some therapies could improve these co-occurring symptoms, but not the core deficit. In other words, it is important not to think that they are necessarily going to improve reading and writing.

Second, many children with dyslexia have lost motivation by the time their parents seek other approaches. Family stress may also be high. It follows that a short-term improvement in the symptoms of dyslexia may be seen as the result of a 'placebo effect' (a beneficial effect driven by the patient's belief that a treatment is working, rather than its actual efficacy), though these will usually be disappointing in the longer term. When an intervention has not been subjected to a robust evaluation process, many factors can be at play, and we will not necessarily know whether or why something works.

Working memory training

Among the cardinal features of dyslexia is a verbal short-term memory problem. People with dyslexia find it hard to remember items in the short term (over a few seconds) but this should not be confused with having poor working memory. Working memory refers to the ability to hold and manipulate information in a limited-capacity 'working space', and involves operations beyond those involved in coding the information verbally (which is where people with dyslexia have their primary difficulty). In contrast, people with ADHD have working memory problems without necessarily having verbal short-term memory problems. A priori, there is no reason to think that children with dyslexia need working memory training.

Working memory training is typically computer-based and involves regular (usually daily) exercises to train auditory and visual memory across modalities through games that challenge the child to work at a higher and higher level. The use of working memory training has been very popular in recent years. However, a comprehensive meta-analysis of the efficacy of such training on academic skills shows that there is no evidence that 'near' gains in trained memory skills transfer to meaningful educational progress. Marketing claims that working memory training improves reading simply cannot be substantiated.

Training in auditory or motor skills

Training programmes to improve basic perceptual and/or motor skills have also been proposed as interventions for dyslexia. The rationale here is that such impairments underlie the phonological deficits that are observed. As we have already seen, there is no strong evidence for the causal theory that deficits in auditory skills lead to reading problems; nor is there a basis in a causal theory to believe that training motor skills will improve reading and spelling attainments.

Nonetheless, auditory training programmes have been developed and some are in use by parents and schools despite the lack of efficacy and the financial costs to the clients. Auditory skills training challenges children in activities aimed at improving the discrimination, sequencing, and memory of speech and non-speech sounds delivered at different rates of presentation. Such training regimes can be effective for improving auditory processing skills but randomized controlled trials have shown that such improvement does not lead to improved reading or spelling skills. In one such study, Fast ForWord®, which uses acoustically modified speech to circumvent assumed difficulties with auditory processing, was compared with an academic enrichment programme and two other forms of language intervention, one computer assisted and one individualized. All children in this study improved on a language task from pre-test to post-intervention but there was no advantage of the programme which used modified speech over the others.

Similarly, and unsurprisingly, there is no evidence for the efficacy of motor skills training for dyslexia. Motor skills training can include activities to improve balance, eye–hand coordination, ball skills, and so on. There is no evidence that this form of training or other physical regimes improve the core symptoms of dyslexia though targeted activities may be useful to help develop pencil control and handwriting skills, which are sometimes affected.

Coloured lenses and overlays

Rather than targeting a deficient cognitive process, a different approach to intervention is to provide an external aid or 'prop' that can overcome a supposed barrier to reading. If someone with dyslexia complains of eye strain, headaches, or other unpleasant visual symptoms during reading, it is reasonable to try to provide a remedy. Normally, this will mean dampening the visual effects that black stripes have on a white background on a page or a computer screen.

For many years, the provision of coloured lenses to reduce visual stress in people with dyslexia was regarded with scepticism, and the costs were considerable. It is now recognized that this is an unnecessary expense; a cheaper alternative is to use coloured filters as overlays on the page, or, if reading from a computer screen, to modify the contrast and/or colour of the background to reduce glare. Provision of an overlay may bring some short-term relief, and it might be useful for a range of conditions, including, but not specifically, dyslexia. However, its impact on reading (as opposed to scanning text) has not been evaluated using robust methods and it is unlikely to help spelling.

Fish oil and dietary supplements

Interventions that target nutrition have gained some popularity. The primary example is omega-3 fish oil which provides fatty acids that contribute to the brain's weight. The rationale here is that a deficiency of these acids will affect brain function and therefore that supplementing the diet with fish oil will improve brain function and hence ameliorate reading and spelling difficulties. There have been very few controlled evaluations of this approach and those which have been completed do not focus specifically on dyslexia. There is also an absence of evidence for interventions that aim to remove certain products or additives from the diet.

One point should be emphasized: the target of nutritional interventions is far removed from the locus of the behaviour where change is desired—in this case reading. It follows that the effects could be small at best (and where there appear to be improvements it is usually because other interventions have been introduced at around the same time).

Is early intervention the answer?

We now know quite a lot about the risk factors for dyslexia. Arguably, this should allow earlier and better targeted interventions. As we have seen, aspects of the home literacy environment can influence the first steps into literacy. Only a small number of studies have investigated the efficacy of intervention for preschool children at family risk of dyslexia. The main approach has been to provide teaching to strengthen the foundations of word decoding by working on phonological awareness and letter knowledge. In one study, this type of intervention was supplemented with work on oral language skills, such as vocabulary and narrative, and a method called 'dialogic reading' has also been used with some success. In dialogic reading, the child and the adult reader 'read a book together' and the adult prompts the child with questions about the story as it unfolds to create a dialogue. Although the results are promising in that children go to school better prepared, the follow-up results from one or two years later are disappointing, suggesting that interventions need to be sustained if 'at-risk' readers are to keep up with their peers.

Notwithstanding this, there is a growing body of evidence suggesting that early interventions delivered by trained teaching assistants can be effective in promoting the foundations of literacy in children at high risk of dyslexia associated with poor oral language at school entry. In the *Nuffield Reading for Language Project* which began in 2004, our group investigated the efficacy of training 5-year-old children in phonological awareness and emergent reading skills during the first year of formal reading instruction. The study was a randomized controlled trial with children allocated to receive either a Reading and Phonology (R+P) programme or a similarly structured Oral Language (OL) Intervention. The content of the R+P programme was based largely on the successful Sound Linkage Programme described earlier, adapted for the younger age group. It comprised three main components: letter-sound work, segmenting and blending, reading together, and reading independently. It was delivered daily for twenty weeks alternating between small group and one-to-one sessions. Four children worked together in a group on letter-sound knowledge, segmenting, and blending and in the individual sessions the work focused on reading, incorporating time to reinforce work on letters and sounds.

The Oral Language Intervention (see Figure 27 and Box 3) was designed to match the R+P programme as far as possible in structure and timing: it was delivered by the same teaching assistants, alternating between individual and group sessions for twenty weeks. The intervention had three main components: vocabulary, listening comprehension, and narrative. Each group session opened with work on listening skills before new vocabulary was introduced using all modalities (seeing a picture, listening to the definition, repeating the word, taking turns to say the word in different contexts); in addition each session had a sequencing, listening, or speaking exercise and the children were encouraged to ask questions. The individual sessions offered an opportunity to revise and consolidate new vocabulary and to work on improving children's storytelling (narrative) skills. Here the

111

child would tell a story, usually depicted in a short cartoon, and the teaching assistant would make a recording of what the child said. Later the transcript was used to extract a teaching point for the next session, for example, to work on verb tense, connectives, or adjectives in order to improve the quality of the narrative.

To identify children to participate in the study, we screened all of the children entering twenty schools in Yorkshire that year and selected in each school the eight children with the weakest performance on tests of expressive naming and recalling

27. **Main components of the published version of the Oral Language Intervention Programme, the Nuffield Early Language Intervention (Oxford, 2018).**

Box 3. Components of intervention

Phonology with Reading Programme	Oral Language Programme
Letter-sound knowledge	Speaking
Oral phonological awareness	Listening
Phonics	Vocabulary
Sight word learning	Narrative production
Reading easy book	Comprehension
Reading book at instructional level	Question generation

sentences. Four of these children were allocated at random to receive the R+P programme and four to receive the OL programme. This was a conservative assessment of the programme: all children were receiving phonics-based reading instruction in the mainstream classroom, it included a treated 'control' group, and children in both arms of the study received a lot of extra attention.

To evaluate the efficacy of the training they received, the gains of the children in the R+P programme on tests of reading and reading-related skills were compared to those of the group who received the oral language work. They were significantly ahead of the children who had received language work in phoneme awareness, prose-reading accuracy, non-word reading, and spelling at the end of the study, and at follow-up some five months later, indicating that the programme had been effective in promoting early reading skills. Furthermore, comparison of the outcomes of these children with those of a large sample of 700 of their classroom peers indicated that more than 50 per cent were performing within the average range for early word reading skills.

This trial also provided proof in principle that oral language training could be delivered by trained teaching assistants: our study found that the OL intervention led to gains in vocabulary and grammar though it was unclear if these would generalize beyond the taught activities. We also reasoned that, if oral language is the foundation for learning to read, then it would be a good idea to start this form of intervention earlier, even perhaps in preschool. In our next study, we delivered an extended (thirty-week) version of the oral language programme to 4-year-old children in the term before they started school and continued it for two further terms after school entry.

Following a similar screening process to before, but with children in UK nursery school settings, we randomly assigned children with poorly developed language skills to receive either a thirty-week oral language programme or to be in a control group who received 'business as usual'. The programme comprised three main components: work on oral narrative, vocabulary, and listening skills. In nursery school, the activities were delivered to groups of two to four children, three times a week. In Reception class, the intensity of the programme was increased to three thirty-minute sessions a week and two fifteen-minute individual sessions in which narrative skills were the focus. In the final ten weeks, the sessions were supplemented with work on letter-sound knowledge and phonological awareness.

Following the intervention, the children who had received the language intervention showed improvements in vocabulary, narrative skills, and listening comprehension as well as in expressive grammar. There was also an impact on their emergent reading on tests of letter knowledge, alliteration matching, and phonetic spelling ability.

Although there was no significant impact of the oral language work on decoding per se, it needs to be borne in mind that this was not the focus of the current intervention. Furthermore, the control group had been receiving instruction in systematic phonics in the mainstream classroom. Despite this, and very importantly, six months later the children who had received the language intervention were ahead of their peers in reading comprehension. Reading comprehension had not been targeted in the intervention, therefore this effect must have been a by-product of the work on oral language skills. A statistical model of the impact of the intervention confirmed that this was the case: gains in reading comprehension were fully accounted for by gains in language skills (and not by gains in word-level decoding abilities). What this means is that a focus on oral language in the early school years can have benefits beyond speaking and listening and can support the development of reading for meaning, a critical aspect of emergent literacy.

What can parents do?

Parents will often be the first to become concerned about their child's progress in reading and writing. If their concerns are not listened to, or no action is taken, they are also the first to become stressed and anxious. The danger then is that they are badged as 'anxious parents' and the problem is shifted from the child to the adult. In my experience, a worried parent is rarely wrong; they will have made comparisons with children of the same age and other children in the family as well as seeking informal advice. They will also witness at first hand their child's emotional reaction to their learning difficulty, be it frustration or upset, and this can often be hidden at school.

A parent or carer's first role is to be an advocate for their child. Their second role is to listen to the professionals with regard to their child's needs and sometimes to provide specific support under the guidance of a teacher or therapist. A third role is to encourage the child to develop in areas of strength—music, art, sport, and drama—and to ensure extra tuition or extra homework doesn't take the place of this. Finally, it is important to remember that parents are not their children's teachers in any formal sense; in the end you have to be 'mum' or 'dad'—have fun, retain a sense of humour, and have realistic expectations. A child with dyslexia may well underachieve academically—indeed, they are quite likely to do so—but it is support in other areas, including social support from peers, which will provide them with much needed emotional resilience.

What can schools do?

Schools and their leaders play critical roles in supporting children with dyslexia. They have responsibilities not least in relation to the assessment, monitoring, and delivery of interventions. They also need to ensure that there is equity in provision such that pupils with dyslexia have the appropriate arrangements in place to allow them to access the curriculum and to be fairly assessed. A teacher responsible for special needs will also need to keep abreast of developments in relation to intervention and assistive technology. According to recent reports, 85 per cent of 9–16-year-olds in Europe use the internet for schoolwork and children are now reading more on electronic devices than print materials. The implications for dyslexia have not yet been researched although there is some limited evidence that e-readers may be beneficial because font size can be manipulated and different formats may be helpful (e.g. shorter lines of text).

Schools should not feel that they act alone. For more complex cases of dyslexia, schools may suggest the involvement of other professionals, such as speech and language or occupational therapists, to assist in the development of health and educational plans. Sometimes further referral may be appropriate and schools play a vital role in signposting to parents how to gain support with attention or behaviour problems which impinge on the family as well as the child in school.

What can employers do?

For adults the landscape of intervention is different. More often than not, they are looking for workplace arrangements which enable them to do their job well (see Figure 28). Diversity in the workplace brings different perspectives and often different skills to the team, and is enriching. The Equality Act (2000) legally protects people from discrimination in the workplace and this includes people with dyslexia. In a case reported in the UK media in 2008, a trainee police officer won £25,000 in compensation after being sacked from the force on account of his dyslexia. Good employers will ensure the needs of employees with dyslexia are met and this may require specialist assessment so that reasonable adjustments can be made. It is in everyone's interests for an individual with dyslexia to disclose their difficulties to a new employer. Often there is a reluctance to do this; that is when things can go wrong. In fact, it went wrong for Harry, who was dismissed from a previous job because of inconsistent administration. He had no recourse because he had not declared his disability.

Promoting 'defences' for dyslexia

Despite the enormous literature on dyslexia, we still know far too little about how best to remediate it. A pessimistic view is that it is not remediable. To some extent that is true—it is a lifelong condition. But there are certainly ways of managing it and these begin with identifying the risk of the problem and providing early intervention. We still don't know how early. I do not advocate formal reading instruction before school entry but spoken language is certainly important. Perhaps one of the best ways of enriching language development is to spend regular time reading age-appropriate books (including pre-reading books for very young children) and discussing the stories with children. Games involving sound play—rhymes and alliteration, and 'I spy'—can help the child tune into the sounds of speech that will be needed

28. An adult literacy group: a medieval woodcut showing a teacher and students.

to develop phonological awareness. It is also helpful to teach a child their letters before they go to school and there is evidence that reading readiness can be promoted by parents if they are properly supported.

For the child in school, monitoring, assessment, and intervention are intricately linked. When interventions fail to make a difference, compensatory strategies should be considered. There is a wealth of educational technology that can help a child with dyslexia but it is important to remember they need to be taught how to use such devices effectively. The same goes for more standard solutions—pupils with dyslexia benefit from being allocated extra time—but how are they going to use it? Pupils can produce better work if they do an essay plan. But this may not come easily to a child with dyslexia who has had little practice with extended writing to date. The great dyslexia educator, Margaret Byrd Rawson, strongly believed that 'if a child can't learn, you are not teaching properly!' For her, the onus for success was on the teacher, not the child.

Chapter 7
The three Cs: caveats, comorbidities, and compensation

Having reached this point, the reader might be wondering why it has been claimed that dyslexia is a myth! The issue at stake is that dyslexia is not a 'category'—it exists on a continuum. Even if it is difficult to be precise about the criteria for defining dyslexia (just as it would be hard to give hard and fast rules for the diagnosis of obesity) there are strong theoretical and moral grounds to use the label 'dyslexia' to refer to people with severe and persistent reading difficulties. Moreover, 'naming it' dyslexia is justified on the grounds of a large body of empirical evidence.

'A rose between two thorns': a working definition of dyslexia

In 2009, Sir Jim Rose published *Identifying and Teaching Children and Young People with Dyslexia and Literacy Difficulties*. This independent review for the UK government drew on the best evidence and practice surrounding the nature and remediation of dyslexia and took into account many hundreds of submissions from parents, teachers, and other stakeholders. After grappling with the problem of definition, the review group proposed a five-point working definition as a conceptual framework to bring together the teaching of literacy to all children with interventions for dyslexia. The definition attracted international interest and commendation; it will be used here as a way of summarizing the important themes running through this book.

> 'Dyslexia primarily affects the skills involved in accurate and fluent word reading and spelling'

No one would disagree with this part of the definition, chiming as it does with that of the American Psychiatric Association's *Diagnostic and Statistical Manual of the Mental Disorders*, known as DSM-5. Although DSM-5 is not used in educational circles, it is the reference 'bible' for clinicians on both sides of the Atlantic. In DSM-5, dyslexia is classified under the category of Specific Learning Disorder; it is one of the neurodevelopmental disorders with onset in childhood which affect reading, written expression, and/or mathematics, with dyslexia an 'alternative term' to refer to 'a pattern of learning difficulties characterized by problems with accurate or fluent word recognition, poor decoding and poor spelling'. DSM-5 also proposes three levels of severity:

mild—fairly well compensated when appropriate arrangements are in place;

moderate—requiring periods of more intense intervention and accommodations;

severe—usually affecting several academic skills and even with interventions causing difficulties in functioning especially during the school years.

These are helpful for considering who needs specialist support and who will be able to function adequately in school or in the workplace when appropriate allowances are made.

> 'Characteristic features of dyslexia are difficulties in phonological awareness, verbal memory and verbal processing speed'

121

The second aspect of the Rose definition describes key aspects of dyslexia's behavioural profile and provides insight into its possible causes. Put another way, the phonological deficit in dyslexia is a difficulty in phonological awareness which compromises the acquisition of reading (and spelling) directly. We have seen that this phonological deficit is universal, and across languages (even in Chinese) awareness of speech is a predictor of individual differences in reading development. It follows from this that a phonological deficit will impede the process of learning to read.

Limitations of verbal short-term memory are a well-known feature of dyslexia. Verbal memory requires language input and speech output and draws on some of the same mechanisms used in reading for translating print into speech. Some years ago, Charles Hulme and I described a severely dyslexic child, 'JM', who was highly intelligent with an excellent vocabulary but could neither read nor repeat nonwords and his spelling was extremely poor. He had a verbal memory span of only two items. As an adult, he told me that 'reading isn't a problem but I struggle to remember what I have been asked to do at work'. Lastly, there is a large body of evidence showing that deficits in verbal processing, detectable using rapid naming tasks, are also a universal marker of a dyslexic difficulty.

'Dyslexia occurs across the range of intellectual abilities; it is best thought of as a continuum, not a distinct category, and there are no clear cut-off points'

The discrepancy definition of dyslexia is no longer in use. Thus it is no longer defined by a discrepancy between IQ-expected reading skill and actual reading level. The graph in Figure 29 shows the normal distribution of reading skill and the percentage of people expected to be defined as 'dyslexic' given different cut-off criteria. It serves as a reminder that dyslexia is a dimension and there is no clear cut-off for 'diagnosis'.

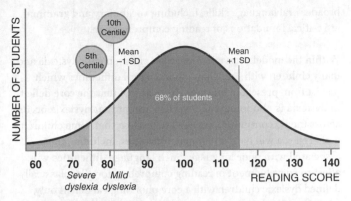

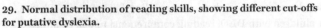

29. Normal distribution of reading skills, showing different cut-offs for putative dyslexia.

In research circles, dyslexia status is often taken as falling below average for age in reading by at least one standard deviation. Arguably, this is a lenient cut because it includes 16 per cent of the population; some research studies use 1.5 standard deviations below average—a score below which only 7 per cent of the population do worse. In contrast, many education authorities set the cut-off point at the 5th centile (only 5 per cent of children would do worse) before a child will receive specialist support. Given the impact of poor literacy on attainment and well-being, this is harsh: using this cut-off, many children who require assistance will not receive it.

There is a further complication. Underlying the reading continuum are other important dimensions, one being spoken language, which is at its foundation. Our synthesis of evidence on the relationship between dyslexia and developmental language disorder (DLD) argued that dyslexia and DLD share common risk factors for poor reading. The findings of the Wellcome Language and Reading Project have subsequently confirmed that this is the case. At the core of learning to read words are phonological aspects of language, such as phonological awareness. However,

123

broader oral language skills, including vocabulary and grammar, are critical foundations of reading comprehension.

Within the model shown in Figure 30, children with dyslexia and many children with DLD have phonological difficulties which persist from preschool onwards. If we accept that the core deficit in dyslexia is phonology, and we also accept that dyslexia occurs across the IQ continuum, we need to be clear that some children with dyslexia will have additional difficulties, including those associated with poor language. Such language difficulties will affect the development of reading comprehension. For classically defined dyslexic children with a core phonological deficit only, poor decoding is the obstacle to reading for meaning, whereas for children with DLD, reading comprehension will be affected regardless of decoding skill. In short, if a child with dyslexia also has poor language, they will need support with reading

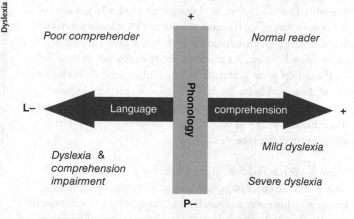

30. **Model of the relationship between dyslexia and developmental language disorder (DLD) after Bishop and Snowling (2004). Children with DLD are on the left of the figure—some have dyslexia, some do not, but all have reading comprehension problems. 'Poor comprehenders' are children who can read well but are vulnerable to failure because their reading comprehension problems can go unnoticed.**

comprehension as well as decoding. This brings us to the issue of comorbidity.

> 'Co-occurring difficulties may be seen in aspects of language, motor co-ordination, mental calculation, concentration and personal organization, but these are not, by themselves, markers of dyslexia'

Comorbidity is a medical term which is used when one or more diseases occur together with a primary disease. The term has been adopted by dyslexia researchers to denote the fact that neurodevelopmental disorders frequently co-occur to the extent that it is often said that 'comorbidity is the norm'. Two different forms of 'comorbidity' are of interest to us here. First, when one disorder is the forerunner of another and precedes it in time. An example is when a child with developmental language disorder (DLD) becomes dyslexic (a causal relation); second, when two distinct disorders coexist at the same time. For example, the same child can experience two distinct disorders, such as dyslexia and developmental coordination disorder (dyspraxia) (an associative relation).

Just as dyslexia is dimensional, so are other neurodevelopmental disorders: the Rose Review refers to language difficulties and motor coordination difficulties rather than the categorical terms 'developmental language disorder' and 'dyspraxia'. Similarly, it refers to mental calculation, concentration, and personal organization rather than dyscalculia and ADHD. The important point is that although none of these difficulties are *central* to the definition or diagnosis of dyslexia, the presence of one or more can complicate how an individual with dyslexia is affected.

Another way of thinking about this is in terms of shared risk factors: poor phonology is a risk factor for poor reading—this is seen in children at family risk of dyslexia and also in children with preschool language difficulties; poor verbal memory is a risk factor for poor mathematical attainment shared between dyscalculia and dyslexia. Some dyslexic children have poor phonology and poor verbal memory so it is not surprising that around 45 per cent of children with dyslexia also have poor language and around 45 per cent have poor numeracy.

The flip side of comorbidity is compensation. Whereas comorbidities can exacerbate the impact of dyslexia, compensatory resources can help ameliorate it. Thus, we have argued that poor readers with good language can use sentence context to help them decode: if they initially sound out '*stomach*' as 'stommatch' but have the word 'stomach' in their vocabulary and know that it is something to do with the body, they are more likely to read it accurately in a sentence such as 'John was off school as he had stomach ache' than a child who doesn't know the word. To take another example, a child who can concentrate well is more likely to learn effectively and, if they have good visual skills, this can help them learn and memorize spellings.

> 'A good indication of the severity and persistence of dyslexic difficulties can be gained by examining how the individual responds or has responded to well-founded intervention'

The starting point for a theoretically well-founded intervention is a causal model of the deficit. The primary cause of dyslexia is a phonological deficit and therefore it is essential to choose an intervention which fosters the phonological skills that are directly related to decoding. However, we know from controlled trials that training in phonological awareness alone is insufficient. The most successful interventions also include components that aim to develop reading fluency, as for example, Hatcher's Reading Intervention in the UK and the multi-componential approaches of Maureen Lovett and her associates in Canada. Critical to all of these effective approaches is monitoring the progress of individual children using response to intervention. Comorbidities complicate the picture and we are yet to understand how best to attend to these in children with dyslexia. There is much ongoing research but as yet no clear solutions.

Multiple risks and multiple pathways

In a landmark paper in 2006, Bruce Pennington reminded us that the causes of disorders like dyslexia are complex and depend on the interaction of multiple genetic and environmental factors. In his multifactorial view, risk and protective factors alter the development of cognitive functions which lead to the behavioural symptoms that define disorders. Importantly, he states that no single deficit is sufficient to explain the development of a disorder. For most of this book, we have taken the phonological deficit as the single deficit at the core of the disorder. However, our consideration of environmental factors, comorbidities, and compensatory resources (including intervention) make clear that there are important caveats to this. These are not the stuff of a very short introduction to dyslexia but there certainly is more than one way you can become dyslexic and, furthermore, there are many different factors that affect the educational attainment and life outcomes of people with dyslexia.

Does this view fit with what is known about the biological bases of dyslexia? We know that many genes of small effect are associated with dyslexia and many of the same genes are associated with related disorders such as ADHD. Even within a 'dyslexic' family, the precise mix of genes differs between individuals and so some family members will receive a bigger hit of genes associated with dyslexia than others. Similarly, genes associated with co-occurring features are distributed among family members.

Figure 31 illustrates how multiple genes might be conceptualized as coding for three different brain profiles, each associated with differing sets of cognitive risks. Such risk factors are sometimes referred to as 'endophenotypes'; these mediate the impact of our biology (genotype) on our behaviour (phenotype). Within the

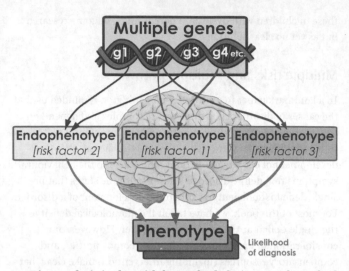

31. Diagram depicting how risk factors for dyslexia accumulate to lead to 'diagnosis'.

figure, the primary risk factor for dyslexia is a phonological deficit. This primary risk can differ in its severity. In addition, there can be additional risk factors that accumulate to increase the severity of dyslexia on a continuum from mild to severe; these may include language difficulties and attentional problems. The figure depicts the hypothesis that the greater the number of risk factors, the greater the likelihood of referral and, hence, diagnosis of a disorder (the phenotype). What the figure does not capture are protective factors; these may include environmental factors, such as teaching and individual differences in 'cognitive resilience'.

Biomarkers of dyslexia?

There is a further piece to the jigsaw and this is at the level of the brain. A common claim is that the left hemisphere language areas underpinning reading show structural and functional differences in dyslexia. In 2002, researchers in Texas reported changes in these same areas following eighty hours of intense intervention in eight children with dyslexia. Before the intervention, the children showed the typical 'dyslexia signature' of reduced activation in posterior left brain with increased activation in similar regions of right brain. At the end of the intervention, activation in the left hemisphere regions had increased and the increases correlated with the improvements in reading skill. These data, while in line with the causal hypothesis of a left hemisphere deficit in dyslexia, are by no means conclusive not least because the sample size was small. Our knowledge of brain systems for compensation is woefully inadequate; we still need to know much more about individual differences in brain structure and function in dyslexia both before and after reading intervention. Correlations such as those reported in the literature do not allow us to unpack causes and consequences and we are a long way from understanding how brain differences in a representative sample of children are related to the well-established cognitive factors causally related to dyslexia. An alternative interpretation of current findings is that differences in learning, both in the early years and after reading instruction, shape the brain itself.

Finally, the word?

A few years ago, an international group of experts got together in the UK to consider once again the research evidence surrounding 'dyslexia' and to debate nomenclature. The outcome of the meeting was to affirm the working definition that Jim Rose had proposed in 2009 and, in particular, to underline the importance of monitoring response to intervention. It seems fitting as a message for policy and practice to reiterate the educational recommendation of the Rose Review: 'all schools...should have access to specialist help with teaching dyslexic pupils'.

Let's finish by returning to the protagonists who have accompanied us on our journey and consider whether the term 'dyslexia' is fitting. Bobby is struggling to learn to read and developing conduct problems. For him, the term 'dyslexia' is the key to gaining the ongoing support he needs and it will help him and others to understand that his frustration is the cause of his behavioural outbursts and that his clowning and misdemeanours are a way of saving face. In the longer term, he should be eligible for appropriate arrangements to be put in place to support his progress in science and maths if he is to pursue a career in one of these fields. For Misha, it is a huge relief to learn that there are reasons why she reads slowly and has spelling problems, and for her teachers to know that she is not just lazy. She is happy to accept that her dyslexia is mild and she is happy just to say she doesn't like maths. A bonus is that she now is less anxious and her motivation to succeed has increased. For both of these children, dyslexia will become part of their identity and an important step in developing resilience in a literate world. Harry has struggled with academic skills throughout his life yet he is successful. Without the strength gained from knowing he is dyslexic, and without the support he received as a result, he does not think he could have achieved his success. He now is seeking support for some of his other difficulties, including his attention problems. People with dyslexia should not need to fail in our education system and parents should not need to fight to have their children's needs recognized. There is strong scientific evidence that dyslexia exists, and research is revealing ways in which individuals with dyslexia differ from one another, and is helping to provide effective interventions. The dyslexia label is an important way of capturing the scientific consensus, and ensuring that children and adults with dyslexia get the support they need—so surely dyslexia should be named.

References

Chapter 1: Does dyslexia exist?

Orton, S. T. (1925). Word blindness in school children. *Archives of Neurology & Psychiatry*, 14(5).

Pringle Morgan, W. (1896). A case of congenital word blindness. *British Medical Journal*, 2(1871), 1378.

Rutter, M., & Yule, W. (1975). The concept of specific reading retardation. *Journal of Child Psychology and Psychiatry*, 16, 181–97.

Chapter 2: How to learn to read (or not)

Byrne, B. (1996). The learnability of the alphabetic principle: children's initial hypotheses about how print represents spoken language. *Applied Psycholinguistics*, 17(4), 401–26.

Hulme, C., Bowyer-Crane, C., Carroll, J. M., Duff, F. J., & Snowling, M. J. (2012). The causal role of phoneme awareness and letter-sound knowledge in learning to read: combining intervention studies with mediation analyses. *Psychological Science*, 23(6), 572–7.

Ehri, L. C. (1995). Phases of development in learning to read words by sight. *Journal of Research in Reading*, 18(2), 116–25.

Jorm, A. F., & Share, D. L. (1983). Phonological recoding and reading acquisition. *Applied Psycholinguistics*, 4(2), 103–47.

Stanovich, K. E. (1980). Toward an interactive-compensatory model of individual differences in the development of reading fluency. *Reading Research Quarterly*, 16(1), 32–71.

Seidenberg, M. S., & McClelland, J. (1989). A distributed, developmental model of word recognition. *Psychological Review*, 96, 523–68.

Treiman, R. (2017). Learning to spell words: findings, theories, and issues. *Scientific Studies of Reading*, *21*(4), 265–76.

Read, C. (1971). Pre-school children's knowledge of English phonology. *Harvard Educational Review*, *41*(1), 1–34.

Caravolas, M., Hulme, C., & Snowling, M. J. (2001). The foundations of spelling ability: evidence from a 3-year longitudinal study. *Journal of Memory and Language*, *45*(4), 751–74.

Treiman, R., Cassar, M., & Zukowski, A. (1994). What types of linguistic information do children use in spelling? The case of flaps. *Child Development*, *65*(5), 1318–37.

Gough, P. B., & Tunmer, W. E. (1986). Decoding, reading, and reading disability. *Remedial and Special Education*, *7*(1), 6–10.

Castles, A., Rastle, K., & Nation, K. (2018). Ending the reading wars: reading acquisition from novice to expert. *Psychological Science in the Public Interest*, *19*(1), 5–51.

Perfetti, C. A., & Hart, L. (2002). The lexical quality hypothesis. *Precursors of Functional Literacy*, *11*, 67–86.

Share, D. L. (2008). On the Anglocentricities of current reading research and practice: the perils of overreliance on an 'outlier' orthography. *Psychological Bulletin*, *134*(4), 584.

Caravolas, M., Lervåg, A., Mousikou, P., Efrim, C., Litavsky, M., Onochie-Quintanilla, E., Hulme, C. (2012). Common patterns of prediction of literacy development in different alphabetic orthographies. *Psychological Science*, *23*(6), 678–86.

Caravolas, M., Lervåg, A., Defior, S., Seidlová Málková, G., Hulme, C. (2013). Different patterns, but equivalent predictors, of growth in reading in consistent and inconsistent orthographies. *Psychological Science*, *24*(8), 1398–407. doi: 10.1177/0956797612473122.

Pan, J., Song, S., Su, M., McBride, C., Liu, H., Zhang, Y., & Shu, H. (2016). On the relationship between phonological awareness, morphological awareness and Chinese literacy skills: evidence from an 8-year longitudinal study. *Developmental Science*, *19*(6), 982–91.

Snowling, M., & Hulme, C. (1989). A longitudinal case study of developmental phonological dyslexia. *Cognitive Neuropsychology*, *6*(4), 379–401.

Chapter 3: What are the cognitive causes of dyslexia?

Wagner, R. K., & Torgeson, J. K. (1987). The nature of phonological processing and its causal role in the acquisition of reading skills. *Psychological Bulletin*, *101*, 192–212.

Lervåg, A., & Hulme, C. (2009). Rapid automatized naming (RAN) taps a mechanism that places constraints on the development of early reading fluency. *Psychological Science*, *20*(8), 1040–8.

Hulme, C., Nash, H. M., Gooch, D., Lervåg, A., & Snowling, M. J. (2015). The foundations of literacy development in children at familial risk of dyslexia. *Psychological Science*, *26*(12), 1877–86.

Vellutino, F. R., Fletcher, J. M., Snowling, M. J., & Scanlon, D. M. (2004). Specific reading disability (dyslexia): what have we learned in the past four decades? *Journal of Child Psychology & Psychiatry*, *45*(1), 2–40.

Hulme, C. (2014). *Reading Retardation and Multi-Sensory Teaching (Psychology Revivals)*. Routledge.

Shankweiler, D., Liberman, I. Y., Mark, L. S., Fowler, C. A., & Fischer, F. W. (1979). The speech code and learning to read. *Journal of Experimental Psychology: Human Learning and Memory*, *5*(6), 531–45.

Snowling, M. J. (1980). The development of grapheme-phoneme correspondence in normal and dyslexic readers. *Journal of Experimental Child Psychology*, *29*(2), 294–305.

Melby-Lervåg, M., Lyster, S.-A. H., & Hulme, C. (2012). Phonological skills and their role in learning to read: a meta-analytic review. *Psychological Bulletin*, *138*(2), 322–52.

Ehri, L. C., & Wilce, L. S. (1980). The influence of orthography on readers' conceptualization of the phonemic structure of words. *Applied Psycholinguistics*, *1*(4), 371–85.

Castro-Caldas, A., Petersson, K. M., Reis, A., Stone-Elander, S., & Ingvar, M. (1998). The illiterate brain: learning to read and write during childhood influences the functional organization of the adult brain. *Brain: A Journal of Neurology*, *121*(6), 1053–63.

Tallal, P. (1980). Auditory temporal perception, phonics, and reading disabilities in children. *Brain and Language*, *9*(2), 182–98.

Snowling, M. J., Gooch, D., McArthur, G., & Hulme, C. (2018). Language skills, but not frequency discrimination, predict reading skills in children at risk of dyslexia. *Psychological Science*, *29*(8), 1270–82.

Goswami, U. (2011). A temporal sampling framework for developmental dyslexia. *Trends in Cognitive Sciences*, *15*(1), 3–10.

Lovegrove, W., Martin, F., & Slaghuis, W. (1986). A theoretical and experimental case for a visual deficit in specific reading disability. *Cognitive Neuropsychology*, *3*(2), 225–67.

Olulade, O. A., Napoliello, E. M., & Eden, G. F. (2013). Abnormal visual motion processing is not a cause of dyslexia. *Neuron*, *79*(1), 180–90.

Bosse, M. L., Tainturier, M. J., & Valdois, S. (2007). Developmental dyslexia: the visual attention span deficit hypothesis. *Cognition*, *104*(2), 198–230.

Ziegler, J. C., Pech-Georgel, C., Dufau, S., & Grainger, J. (2010). Rapid processing of letters, digits and symbols: what purely visual-attentional deficit in developmental dyslexia? *Developmental Science*, *13*(4), F8–14.

Rochelle, K. S., & Talcott, J. B. (2006). Impaired balance in developmental dyslexia? A meta-analysis of the contending evidence. *Journal of Child Psychology and Psychiatry*, *47*(11), 1159–66.

Saksida, A., Iannuzzi, S., Bogliotti, C., Chaix, Y., Démonet, J. F., Bricout, L.,... & Ramus, F. (2016). Phonological skills, visual attention span, and visual stress in developmental dyslexia: insights from a population of French children. *Developmental Psychology*, *52*(10), 1503–16.

Snowling, M. J., & Melby-Lervåg, M. (2016). Oral language deficits in familial dyslexia: a meta-analysis and review. *Psychological Bulletin*, *142*(5), 498–545.

Pennington, B. F. (2006). From single to multiple deficit models of developmental disorders. *Cognition*, *101*(2), 385–413.

Snowling, M. J., Nash, H. M., Gooch, D., Hayiou-Thomas, M. E., Hulme, C., and the Wellcome Language and Reading Team (2019). Developmental outcomes of children at high risk of dyslexia and developmental language disorder. *Child Development*. https://doi.org/10.1111/cdev.13216

Chapter 4: Dyslexia genes and the environment—a class act?

Sonuga-Barke, E. J. (2010). 'It's the environment stupid!' On epigenetics, programming and plasticity in child mental health. *Journal of Child Psychology and Psychiatry*, *51*(2), 113–15.

Bronfenbrenner, U. (1977). Toward an experimental ecology of human development. *American Psychologist*, *32*(7), 513–31.

Sénéchal, M., & LeFevre, J.-A. (2002). Parental involvement in the development of children's reading skill: a five-year longitudinal study. *Child Development*, *73*(2), 445–60.

Dilnot, J., Hamilton, L., Maughan, B., & Snowling, M. J. (2017). Child and environmental risk factors predicting readiness for learning in children at high risk of dyslexia. *Development and Psychopathology*, *29*(1), 235–44.

Chapter 5: The dyslexic brain

Galaburda, A. M., Sherman, G. F., Rosen, G. D., Aboitiz, F., & Geschwind, N. (1985). Developmental dyslexia: four consecutive patients with cortical anomalies. *Annals of Neurology: Official Journal of the American Neurological Association and the Child Neurology Society*, *18*(2), 222–33.

Paulesu, E., Frith, U., Snowling, M., Gallagher, A., Morton, J., Frackowiak, R. S., & Frith, C. D. (1996). Is developmental dyslexia a disconnection syndrome? Evidence from PET scanning. *Brain*, *119*(1), 143–57.

Shaywitz, B. A., Shaywitz, S. E., Pugh, K. R., Fulbright, R. K., Mencl, W. E., Constable, R. T., ... & Gore, J. C. (2001). The neurobiology of dyslexia. *Clinical Neuroscience Research*, *1*(4), 291–9.

Shaywitz, S. E., Shaywitz, B. A., Fulbright, R. K., Skudlarski, P., Mencl, W. E., Constable, R. T., ... & Gore, J. C. (2003). Neural systems for compensation and persistence: young adult outcome of childhood reading disability. *Biological Psychiatry*, *54*(1), 25–33.

Shaywitz, S., & Shaywitz, B. (2008). Paying attention to reading: the neurobiology of reading and dyslexia. *Development and Psychopathology*, *20*(4), 1329–49.

BishopBlog <http://deevybee.blogspot.com/2012/05/neuronal-migration-in-language-learning.html>

Paulesu, E., Démonet, J. F., Fazio, F., McCrory, E., Chanoine, V., Brunswick, N., ... & Frith, U. (2001). Dyslexia: cultural diversity and biological unity. *Science*, *291*(5511), 2165–7.

Hu, W., Lee, H. L., Zhang, Q., Liu, T., Geng, L. B., Seghier, M. L., & Price, C. J. (2010). Developmental dyslexia in Chinese and English populations: dissociating the effect of dyslexia from language differences. *Brain*, *133*(6), 1694–706.

Carreiras, M., Seghier, M. L., Baquero, S., Estévez, A., Lozano, A., Devlin, J. T., & Price, C. J. (2009). An anatomical signature for literacy. *Nature*, *461*(7266), 983.

Hoeft, F., Meyler, A., Hernandez, A., Juel, C., Taylor-Hill, H., Martindale, J., ... & Gabrieli, J. (2007). Functional and morphometric brain dissociation between dyslexia and reading ability. *Proceedings of the National Academy of Sciences of the United States of America*, *104*(10), 4234–9.

References

Hoeft, F., Hernandez, A., Taylor-Hill, H., Martindale, J. L., Meyler, A., Keller, T. A., . . . & Gabrieli, J. D. (2006). Neural basis of dyslexia: a comparison between dyslexic and nondyslexic children equated for reading ability. *The Journal of Neuroscience*, *26*(42), 10700–8.

Hoeft, F., McCandliss, B. D., Black, J. M., Gantman, A., Zakerani, N., Hulme, C., . . . & Gabrieli, J. D. (2011). Neural systems predicting long-term outcome in dyslexia. *Proc Natl Acad Sci USA*, *108*(1), 361–6.

Molfese, D. L. (2000). Predicting dyslexia at 8 years of age using neonatal brain responses. *Brain and Language*, *72*(3), 238–45.

Chapter 6: What works for dyslexia?

Rose Review <https://www.gov.uk/government/publications/letters-and-sounds>

Duff, F. J., Mengoni, S. E., Bailey, A. M., & Snowling, M. J. (2015). Validity and sensitivity of the phonics screening check: implications for practice. *Journal of Research in Reading*, *38*(2), 109–23.

Hatcher, P., Hulme, C., & Ellis, A. W. (1994). Ameliorating early reading failure by integrating the teaching of reading and phonological skills: the phonological linkage hypothesis. *Child Development*, *65*, 41–57.

Vygotsky, L. (1987). Zone of proximal development. *Mind in Society: The Development of Higher Psychological Processes*, *5291*, 157.

Cumbria Reading Intervention <http://www.cumbria.gov.uk/childrensservices/schoolsandlearning/reading/default.asp>

Frith, U. (2017). Beneath the surface of developmental dyslexia. In *Surface Dyslexia* (pp. 301–30). Routledge.

Duff, F. J., Fieldsend, E., Bowyer-Crane, C., Hulme, C., Smith, G., Gibbs, S., & Snowling, M. J. (2008). Reading with vocabulary intervention: evaluation of an instruction for children with poor response to reading intervention. *Journal of Research in Reading*, *31*(3), 319–36.

Melby-Lervåg, M., & Hulme, C. (2013). Is working memory training effective? A meta-analytic review. *Developmental Psychology*, *49*(2), 270–91.

Gillam, R. B., Loeb, D. F., Hoffman, L. M., Bohman, T., Champlin, C. A., Thibodeau, L., . . . & Friel-Patti, S. (2008). The efficacy of Fast ForWord language intervention in school-age children with language impairment: a randomized controlled trial. *Journal of Speech, Language, and Hearing Research*, *51*(1), 97–119.

Bowyer-Crane, C., Snowling, M. J., Duff, F. J., Fieldsend, E., Carroll, J. M., Miles, J., Götz, K., & Hulme, C. (2008). Improving early language and literacy skills: differential effects of an oral language versus a phonology with reading intervention. *Journal of Child Psychology and Psychiatry*, *49*, 422–32.

Fricke, S., Bowyer-Crane, C., Haley, A., Hulme, C., & Snowling, M. J. (2013). Building a secure foundation for literacy: an evaluation of a preschool language intervention. *Journal of Child Psychology and Psychiatry*, *54*, 280–90.

Equality Act 2000 <https://www.gov.uk/guidance/equality-act-2010-guidance> (accessed 6 August 2018).

Rawson, M. B. (1995). *Dyslexia over the Lifespan: A Fifty-Five Year Longitudinal Study*. Educators Pub. Services.

Chapter 7: The three Cs: caveats, comorbidities, and compensation

Rose, J. (2009). Identifying and teaching children and young people with dyslexia and literacy difficulties. Retrieved 28 December, 2009, from <http://webarchive.nationalarchives.gov.uk/20091004042342/http://www.dcsf.gov.uk/jimroseanddyslexia/>

American Psychiatric Association (2013). *The Diagnostic and Statistical Manual of Mental Disorders*, DSM5.

Snowling, M., & Hulme, C. (1989). A longitudinal case study of developmental phonological dyslexia. *Cognitive Neuropsychology*, *6*(4), 379–401.

Bishop, D. V., & Snowling, M. J. (2004). Developmental dyslexia and specific language impairment: same or different? *Psychological Bulletin*, *130*(6), 858–86.

Hatcher, P. J., Duff, F. J., & Hulme, C. (2014). *Sound Linkage: An Integrated Programme for Overcoming Reading Difficulties*. John Wiley & Sons.

Lovett, M. W., Lacerenza, L., Borden, S. L., Frijters, J. C., Steinbach, K. A., & De Palma, M. (2000). Components of effective remediation for developmental reading disabilities: combining phonological and strategy-based instruction to improve outcomes. *Journal of Educational Psychology*, *92*(2), 263–83.

Pennington, B. F. (2006). From single to multiple deficit models of developmental disorders. *Cognition*, *101*(2), 385–413.

Simos, P. G., Fletcher, J. M., Bergman, E., Breier, J. I., Foorman, B. R., Castillo, E. M., . . . & Papanicolaou, A. C. (2002). Dyslexia-specific brain activation profile becomes normal following successful remedial training. *Neurology*, *58*(8), 1203–13.

Further reading

Chapter 1: Does dyslexia exist?

Ramus, F. (2014). Should there really be a 'Dyslexia debate'? *Brain*, *137*(12), 3371–4.

Rutter, M., & Maughan, B. (2005). Dyslexia: 1965–2005. *Behavioural and Cognitive Psychotherapy*, *33*(4), 389–402.

Satz, P., & Fletcher, J. M. (1987). Left-handedness and dyslexia: an old myth revisited. *Journal of Pediatric Psychology*, *12*(2), 291–8.

Chapter 2: How to learn to read (or not)

McBride-Chang, C. (2014). *Children's Literacy Development*. Routledge.

Seidenberg, M. (2017). *Language at the Speed of Sight: How we Read, Why so Many Can't, and What Can Be Done About It*: Basic Books.

Chapter 3: What are the cognitive causes of dyslexia?

Boden, C., & Giaschi, D. (2007). M-stream deficits and reading-related visual processes in developmental dyslexia. *Psychological Bulletin*, *133*(2), 346–66.

Schulte-Körne, G., & Bruder, J. (2010). Clinical neurophysiology of visual and auditory processing in dyslexia: a review. *Clinical Neurophysiology*, *121*(11), 1794–809.

Ziegler, J. C., & Goswami, U. C. (2005). Reading acquisition, developmental dyslexia and skilled reading across languages: a psycholinguistic grain size theory. *Psychological Bulletin*, *131*(1), 3–29.

Chapter 4: Dyslexia genes and the environment—a class act?

Byrne, B., Wadsworth, S., Boehme, K., Talk, A. C., Coventry, W. L., Olson, R. K.,...& Corley, R. (2013). Multivariate genetic analysis of learning and early reading development. *Scientific Studies of Reading*, *17*(3), 224–42.

Friend, A., DeFries, J. C., Olson, R. K., Pennington, B., Harlaar, N., Byrne, B.,...& Corley, R. (2009). Heritability of high reading ability and its interaction with parental education. *Behavior Genetics*, *39*(4), 427–36.

Lyytinen, H., Ahonen, T., Eklund, K., Guttorm, T., Kulju, P., Laakso, M. L., & Richardson, U. (2004). Early development of children at familial risk for dyslexia—follow-up from birth to school age. *Dyslexia*, *10*(3), 146–78.

Newbury, D. F., et al. (2011). Investigation of dyslexia and SLI risk variants in reading- and language-impaired subjects. *Behavior Genetics*, *41*(1): 90–104.

Phillips, B. M., & Lonigan, C. J. (2005). Social correlates of emergent literacy. In M. J. Snowling & C. Hulme (eds), *The Science of Reading: A Handbook* (pp. 173–87). Blackwell.

Rutter, M., & Maughan, B. (2002). School effectiveness findings 1979–2002. *Journal of School Psychology*, *40*(6), 451–75.

Chapter 5: The dyslexic brain

Hämäläinen, J. A., Salminen, H. K., & Leppänen, P. H. T. (2013). Basic auditory processing deficits in dyslexia: systematic review of the behavioral and event-related potential/field evidence. *Journal of Learning Disabilities*, *46*(5), 413–27.

Leppänen, P. H. T., Pihko, E., Eklund, K. M., & Lyytinen, H. (1999). Cortical responses of infants with and without a genetic risk for dyslexia: II. Group effects. *NeuroReport*, *10*, 969–73.

McCrory, E. J., Mechelli, A., Frith, U., & Price, C. J. (2004). More than words: a common neural basis for reading and naming deficits in developmental dyslexia? *Brain*, *128*(2), 261–7.

Chapter 6: What works for dyslexia?

Carroll, J. M., Bowyer-Crane, C., Duff, F., Hulme, C., & Snowling, M. J. (2011). *Developing Language and Literacy: Effective Intervention for Language and Literacy in the Early Years*. Wiley-Blackwell.

Clarke, P. J., Truelove, E., Hulme, C., & Snowling, M. J. (2013). *Developing Reading Comprehension*. Wiley-Blackwell.

Hulme, C., & Melby-Lervåg, M. (2015). Educational interventions for children's learning difficulties. A. Thapar et al. (eds), *Rutter's Child and Adolescent Psychiatry* (pp. 533–44). Wiley.

Nunes, T., Bryant, P., & Olsson, J. (2003). Learning morphological and phonological spelling rules: an intervention study, *Scientific Studies of Reading*, 7(3), 289–307.

Thompson, P. A., Hulme, C., Nash, H. M., Gooch, D., Hayiou-Thomas, E., & Snowling, M. J. (2015). Developmental dyslexia: predicting individual risk. *Journal of Child Psychology and Psychiatry*, 56(9), 976–87.

Vaughn, S., Denton, C. A., & Fletcher, J. M. (2010). Why intensive interventions are necessary for students with severe reading difficulties. *Psychology in the Schools*, 47(5), 432–44.

Chapter 7: The three Cs: caveats, comorbidities, and compensation

Hulme, C., & Snowling, M. J. (2009). *Developmental Disorders of Language, Learning & Cognition*. Wiley-Blackwell.

Moll, K., Göbel, S. M., Gooch, D., Landerl, K., & Snowling, M. J. (2016). Cognitive risk factors for specific learning disorder: processing speed, temporal processing, and working memory. *Journal of Learning Disabilities*, 49(3), 272–81.

Peterson, R. L., & Pennington, B. F. (2015). Developmental dyslexia. *Annual Review of Clinical Psychology*, 11, 283–307.

Index

SOCIAL MEDIA
Very Short Introduction

Join our community

www.oup.com/vsi

- Join us online at the official Very Short Introductions **Facebook** page.
- Access the thoughts and musings of our authors with our online **blog**.
- Sign up for our monthly **e-newsletter** to receive information on all new titles publishing that month.
- Browse the full range of Very Short Introductions online.
- Read **extracts** from the Introductions for free.
- If you are a teacher or lecturer you can order inspection copies quickly and simply via our website.